THE ROYAL SOCIETY OF LITERATURE
A PORTRAIT

THE ROYAL SOCIETY OF LITERATURE

A PORTRAIT

ISABEL QUIGLY

THE ROYAL SOCIETY OF LITERATURE

CAMBRIDGE UNIVERSITY LIBRARY

A catalogue record for this book is available from the
British Library

ISBN 0 90220557 9

First published in 2000 jointly by the
Royal Society of Literature, 3 Johnson's Court,
London EC4 3EA
and
Cambridge University Library, West Road, Cambridge,
CB3 9DR

Printed in Great Britain by Redwood Books, Trowbridge,
BA14 8RN

Book design: Miles Huddleston
Cover: Tom Sawyer
Typesetting: Annie Alexander

In memoriam
R.A.S.

CONTENTS

ILLUSTRATIONS

PREFACE

For many years Cambridge University Library has been strengthening and consolidating its manuscript collections relating to English literature of the nineteenth and twentieth centuries. I am delighted therefore that it should provide a permanent home for the archive of the Royal Society of Literature. The Society's move from Hyde Park Gardens to Somerset House has provided the occasion for its archive, formerly crammed — as Isabel Quigly writes in this book — into cupboards, shelves and boxes, to be rehoused in secure archival conditions, professionally classified and handlisted, and made widely available for scholarly enquiry. Through this major purchase, supported by generous grants from the Museums and Galleries Commission/Victoria and Albert Museum Purchase Grant Fund, the Friends of the National Libraries, and the Friends of Cambridge University Library, the Society's surviving archive has been allowed to remain virtually intact (all but the minute books and the files of living Fellows having been transferred to Cambridge), and so has avoided the fate of certain similar collections from which items of autograph value were dispersed at auction.

Since its foundation in 1820 the Society has been a singular institution in British intellectual life. In its early years, when the term "literature" was very broadly interpreted, the archive garnered material of antiquarian, historical, philosophical and philological interest: papers read before the Society, and surviving in the archive, include

[1]

Joseph Bonomi on obelisks, James Orchard Halliwell on Euclid, and Sir William Ouseley on ancient Arabian calligraphy. In the twentieth century this inclusive tradition persisted in the admission to Fellowship of such authors as the historian Dame Veronica Wedgwood, the scientist Marie Stopes, and the philosopher Bertrand Russell: all are represented in the Society's files. The correspondence in the archive includes letters from Southey, Crabbe and Felicia Hemans from the earliest years of the Society, through Hardy, Yeats and Sassoon in the first half of this century, to Golding, Larkin and Hughes in recent decades. The Society's council and committee members are prominently represented in the archive, and have included literary authors such as Edmund Gosse, Henry Newbolt and Walter de la Mare, and leading public figures like Robert Crewe-Milnes, Marquis of Crewe, and R.A. Butler. The archive is both a detailed record of the Society's administration and achievements, and material for the study of individual authors. It is a valuable source for historians of this country's literary culture, and although hitherto its "private" status has meant that its research value has remained largely unrealised, I expect that this will change quickly now that it is available to scholars in the University Library.

Over the course of the Society's history it has been closely connected with Cambridge alumni. Coleridge was one of the first Royal Associates; A.C. Benson, Master of Magdalene College, endowed the Society's silver medal; and many other members of the University have been leading figures of the Society. Many, indeed, are already extensively represented in the University Library's manuscript collections. Sassoon, Gosse, and Crewe-Milnes may serve as examples. It is a cause of great pleasure that these links have been confirmed and strengthened by the acquisition of the archive.

Peter Fox
Librarian
University of Cambridge

FOREWORD

The Royal Society of Literature has had a curious and fluctuating history of 180 years. For several quite long periods it has coasted along in the shadows, not doing any harm, but not doing a great deal of good either, and certainly not being the focus and forum of the most interesting and influential writers of the time. Alternating with these fallow periods, however, it has had bursts of activity and even fame. It started quite well, with one of its first subventions being to Coleridge, but it then passed a reposeful Victorian age, with the great novelists and the great poets standing determinedly offshore. It mostly had great noblemen for its presidents, but not great writers for its Fellows.

Then in 1910, at the end of the Edwardian afternoon, it suddenly had a burst of renewed vitality. Conrad, Hardy, Henry James, Yeats and many others joined the so-called Academic Committee of the Society. So many of real distinction flooded in that refusals from Housman and Virginia Woolf could be comfortably sustained. (Housman was a great refuser: he even embraced the Order of Merit in his negativism.) While it cannot be said that the Society has sustained that new momentum throughout the whole of this century, it has in recent years had another impression of vigour and faces the millennium in good shape and heart.

Isabel Quigly, who was asked to write a commemorative history of the RSL, has been particularly good at bringing out these fluctuations and ambiguities. She has certainly not written a "chamber of commerce" brochure. There are no bland and false puffs. She has an acute eye for quirky facts and ironic paradoxes. First the RSL has consistently celebrated, not the anniversary of its birth, which was in 1820 and at Hatchards bookshop, but its belated christening, which was in 1825, when it received its royal charter and a good deal of patronage from George IV. This, however, was brought to an abrupt end when he was succeeded by his brother, "the sailor king", and was not much revived during the long Victorian years, even when Prince Albert was alive. It was not until the present Queen attended the (false!) 150th anniversary that the "Royal" of the title assumed any further significance.

Second, the Society in its early days was not much concerned with "literature" in the sense of creative writing. It was much more interested in knowledge and mostly in a dry, antiquarian and clerically-based form. During those years of dryness the Society occupied a fine house built for it in the wake of George IV's generosity by Decimus Burton on the site of what is today the National Portrait Gallery. From 1884, it was more peripatetic, although it has been in Hyde Park Gardens for the past fifty years, just about as long as it was in St Martin's Place, and is now about to move to the architectural splendour of Somerset House.

The Edwardian flowering ran on to the end of 1920, but lost momentum in the 1930s. After the war there was a substantial revival, which has been reinforced in the past decade. To some extent vitality has been measured by the extent to which the Society's own honour, the Companionship of Literature, has been bestowed. Walter Scott, even though he had originally been hostile to the foundation of the Society, was given an early one by his admiring sovereign. Then nothing much happened on this front until Hardy, Meredith and Kipling were honoured together. Shaw was the last of the pre-war Companions in 1939. In 1961 new life (but not new youth) was infused into the order by the simultaneous installation of Winston Churchill, E.M. Forster, Somerset Maugham and John Masefield. Since then the full but strictly limited complement of ten has been kept up, with only short delays. Harold Pinter and D.J. Enright have in 1999 completed the strength.

During the last half century the presidency has been occupied by the disparate trio of Rab Butler, Angus Wilson and myself. But this is largely a non-playing office. The effective leadership comes from the Chairman, and the Society has recently been very lucky to have first John Mortimer and now Michael Holroyd in that rôle.

Roy Jenkins
President
The Royal Society of Literature

ORIGINS

W HAT DID the word "literature", in the sense we now use it, mean in the early nineteenth century? Not much.

When the Royal Society of Literature was founded it was hardly concerned at all with what we now call literature. Yet everyone who joined signed a pledge to work for the advancement of literature, whatever that meant, and the word was used in all the early documents, the constitution, the rules and protocols. What in fact was meant by it, though? According to the OED, the use of the word to mean "writing which has claim to consideration on the ground of beauty of form or emotional effect" is "very recent". But how recent is recent?

The date of its first use in this sense is given as 1812 and it is a scientist, Sir Humphry Davy, who is first credited with thus using it. But in 1820 this was not how the word was generally understood. The early members of the RSL, devoted followers of what they thought of as literature, seem to have had little idea of it as a creative expression of the human spirit, the transference of experience into poetry, drama, fiction or other forms of imaginative writing. Little idea, that is, unless it came out of the ancient European world of Greece and Rome. Classical writing, yes, meant the imaginative work we think of as literature; but what had been written since, the more modern, the vernacular, was not a subject for academic study or for pursuit by the learned. The public schools and those that copied them (which in effect meant nearly all secondary education), and the universities, put classical studies above all others. This meant not just Greek and Latin but ancient history and its culture, the whole framework of the ancient world. On this foundation the educated man (women, being mainly uneducated, were another matter) was expected to base his view of the world, his idea of the past and of philosophy, his culture in general.

English literature was neglected to an extraordinary degree in nineteenth-century education. At the end of the century the universities thought it an entirely new and suspect subject — suspect mainly because it was widely taught in adult education classes and therefore was accessible to everyone. It was considered a soft option, the uneducated equivalent of the (ancient) classics, and at university level likely to lower academic standards. As in all things English, snobbery was involved, extending even to the study of English literature, acknowledged to be the world's greatest. Those who could not afford the time or the school fees to study the Greek and Latin classics could read the English ones, and this was enough to belittle them in the eyes of the more expensively educated. A gentleman must learn Latin "for the confounding of cads". (Was it Lord Chesterfield who said it? It certainly sounds the kind of thing he would have thought.) A cad meant anyone outside the public-school world, and the universities followed the schools in this belief. Apart from the professorship of poetry set up in 1708 and the Merton professorship of English language and literature set up in 1885, the only chair of English at Oxford was that of Anglo Saxon and the English honours school was not established there until 1893. Cambridge was even tardier: as late as the early 1920s.

In the public schools which fed the universities, the teaching of English literature was not part of the curriculum. A boy could go right through his schooldays knowing nothing of his own literature. This is made clear in school stories: a master invites a group of boys round in the evening, and introduces them, to their astonishment and delight, to Keats or the metaphysicals (say), never read or even heard of before. This happens so often in school stories and memoirs that it becomes almost a cliché.

Literature in the nineteenth century was not as clearly divided from the other arts and disciplines as it is now. As it was then considered, it meant simply "writing". This could mean writing about almost anything. At a high level it meant Johnson, Gibbon, Lamb, Macaulay, Carlyle, Arnold; it also meant writers of memoirs and letters and diaries, biographers, historians, essayists, even journalists, and certainly the erudite who wrote on subjects that occupied the RSL in its first 75 years. At a high level this is still the case, but since the first years of the twentieth century the main body of RSL Fellows has consisted of imaginative, creative, personal writers.

There were some advantages in the earlier openness: practitioners in all the arts were drawn to the RSL and the breadth of interests at the beginning must have enriched the whole membership and cross-fertilised its work. Sir Thomas Lawrence brought a painter's eye, Sir Francis Chantrey a sculptor's, John Nash and Decimus Burton the insights of architecture, Henry Fox Talbot the new ways of

[11]

looking at the world which photography was to open up. And at a less eminent, more specialised level there were the scholars, the academics, the experts on this and that, among whom Mr Casaubon of *Middlemarch* would have felt at home: Sir James Frazer, for instance, joined as early as 1899.

Specialists were all very well, and if the RSL had continued to leaven them with more broadly based others, or with men of letters, things might have been different. But after the earliest days, its interests narrowed. For a long time it seems like a coterie of cronies, self-perpetuating because they elected other cronies; made up mainly of worthy mediocrities who appointed others like themselves. The writers of papers which appear in the *Transactions* are often the same ones, over and over again, since the Council appointed the speakers and then chose which papers from among them should be published. Some of these were the eager beavers always found in such groups, anxious to be involved in everything, some (one cannot help thinking) were perhaps social climbers, namedroppers, men about town, ambitious journalists like William Jerdan. Some were serious scholars — Sharon Turner, for instance, the founder of Anglo-Saxon studies — but most have long been forgotten.

In the higher reaches clerics and noblemen were prominent, if not predominant. Dukes were particularly fancied, pursued and occasionally caught for presidential (or at least vice-presidential) positions, and among them royal dukes with the smallest literary pretensions were the favourites. That the RSL was then, like almost everyone else, so much impressed by rank, so eager to involve the aristocracy in its affairs, is hardly surprising in so hierarchical an age. And if social eminence beat literary distinction every time, it must have been to some extent because few writers of distinction had joined the RSL, so that there was little choice of distinguished leaders among them.

Throughout the nineteenth century the great majority of papers read at the RSL were on ancient subjects: as David Williams, historian of those early years, put it, there was "the complete envelopment of the Society by Egyptian, Assyrian, Greek, and Roman antiquities". The index to the *Transactions* (volumes of the supposedly best papers given), a 32-page booklet, is a strange document for a modern literary society. Page after page gives the titles of lectures such as "The Ogham-Runes and El-Mushajjar", "Some Aspects of Zeus and Apollo worship", "Cleon, the Demagogue", "Egyptian Papyrus Literature as illustrated by Recent Discoveries", "The Sporting Literature of Ancient Greece and Rome", "On the Central Groups of the Eastern Frieze of the Parthenon", "The Mummies of the Priest of Ammon discovered at Thebes", "Some Linguistic Synonyms in the Pre-Roman Languages of Britain and Italy", and so on.

A few non-classical, non-academic and non-ancient (though scarcely modern) topics turn up now and then, seemingly haphazard oddments: "A slight mistake of Lord Macaulay", "Medieval libraries", "Place-names in the Crimea", "Snows, Rains and Thermal Springs in Abyssinia". Only in the 1860s do a couple of specifically literary lectures appear, one on Coleridge, the other on Shakespeare. In the 1870s and 1880s, there is more

Shakespeare, and subjects appear that might be called literary, philological or at least cultural: "Errors in speaking and writing", "What is poetry?", a glossary of Cumbrian dialect; Petrarch, Bacon and Herrick, Leonardo da Vinci, Grotius, Rubens, Leo XIII — a very mixed bag.

So classical subjects, though still dominant, were being diluted a little, and more modern (though not yet contemporary) writing was given a small part of the RSL's attention. Then, from the mid-1890s, the papers suddenly change. No more tombs in Mesopotamia, pyramids or papyri; no more geology or geography, archaeology or anthropology. Just over a century ago the Royal Society of Literature began to take an interest in what it had set out to promote, literature.

What happened to bring about this change? The minutes of Council meetings are so discreet that it is impossible to tell exactly. But certainly something took place on 9 January 1895, when a vice-president, Dr Phené, read a paper to the Council containing what seem to have been radical suggestions for change. The minutes say: "We proceeded to discuss the general and special causes of this [the unsatisfactory state of the Society's income]. Passing on to suggestions for improving the general condition, he proposed a modification of the Transactions, consisting in the addition of matters of general literary interest such as a report of the latest works in high class literature, also stereotyped pages of important dates and other facts in literary history. He then proposed the institution of commemorations of great writers in early English history and suggested one in May next in celebration of King Alfred

[14]

and Chaucer." Then, "Mr Brabrook [later Sir Edward] proposed and Mr Ames seconded that a committee be appointed to consider ways and means for giving effect to Dr Phené's proposals."

By the following month the committee had been set up and the Council had approved "in principal the plan laid before them". By the month after that (at the meeting in March 1895), a preliminary circular had been drafted. The turnabout seems dramatically abrupt. From 1895 almost every paper given is literary. The president, Lord Halsbury, speaks on poetry; two vice-presidents on ethical and symbolical literature in art and on English alliteration from Chaucer to Milton; others speak on *Hudibras*, on Nashe, on seventeeth-century drama, Goethe's *Faust*, Tennyson's religious poetry, *Macbeth*, the development of literary criticism in England; in other words on things one might expect to hear about at a literary gathering. Oddly enough, the only old-style paper which appears in the *Transactions* of 1896 is by the innovative Dr Phené: "Tree transporting: researches for an examination of still existing people, languages, customs, and remains mentioned by Herodotus, Strabo, etc., in India, Thrace, Italy and Western Europe." But Dr Phené's suggestion that new books should be noted in the *Transactions* has been taken up and, on three and a half pages, recently published and forthcoming books are listed, and plans for others mentioned. The format is vague, with few hard facts on publishers and dates. But at least it is a beginning: Fellows are made aware of a few things that are happening or are about to happen in the world of letters.

If, as I think it must have been, Dr Phené's plan was for a complete change of direction, then it looks as if he, rather than Bishop Burgess and the founding fathers, should be given credit for what has happened over the past century in the RSL. If it had continued to be a gathering of specialised, learned men rather than creative writers, it would probably have limped along as it was doing in the 1890s, a poor relation of other learned societies, with no clear identity of its own and little literary character. As it was, it gathered strength and momentum throughout the next decade, until it became not just a centre for men (and later women) of letters, but something of a literary powerhouse, attracting most of the best writers and best minds of the time, with ambitious plans, wide interests, influence at home and abroad and respect from the world around it. And it is Dr John Samuel Phené, I think, that we should thank for it.

He was not himself a "modern" man of letters, and the papers he gave at the RSL were on classical subjects, except for his final one, which came closer to the modern age — with Chaucer, not exactly a modern figure. But he opened windows on to the world of letters as we now think of it, and for that, surely, he deserves the recognition he has never had. From that afternoon in 1895 the RSL as we know it seems to have sprung, and within a decade the more literary RSL was attracting the big names in the world of letters and their enthusiastic support.

When Dr Phené made his proposals, Meredith was perhaps the only Fellow who could be called a big name (certainly his was big at the time). He was elected in 1894.

It was in 1907 that Fellows of real distinction arrived: Hardy was obviously the top one among them but others were well worth having, too. Writers of solid reputation, and mostly of some fame, were now ready to work for the resurgence of the Society, men with influence and contacts who gave it the sort of gloss it needed after so many dingy years. In the same year, 1907, came Henry James, Edmund Gosse, Henry Newbolt, and A.C. Benson, among others of some prominence; and two famous foreign Fellows, Fogazzaro and Maeterlinck. The RSL was going up; election had become an honour.

Lists of Fellows for the next eleven years are missing, no one can tell why. The apparently haphazard gaps in the archives cannot be explained, though perhaps, when a more finely-toothed comb has been through them in their new home, more satisfactory answers may be found. The next list I found was printed in 1918, and it shows how much the Fellowship had changed and what a high-powered body the Society had become. With Yeats and Conrad, Shaw and Pinero and Barrie, Galsworthy and Beerbohm, Bridges, Masefield, Binyon and Drinkwater, de la Mare and Alice Meynell, and a further dozen of obvious distinction, it could claim a dominant role in English literary life. Among foreign Fellows were Anatole France and Pierre Loti, Fridtjof Nansen, Palacio Valdés and Perez Galdós, and at home two who were better known for non-literary reasons, Arthur Balfour and the Earl of Lytton, who later became the Society's president. In the next twelve years they were joined by a further thirty-six leading writers who included Chesterton, Sassoon, Buchan, Maugham, Kipling,

Wodehouse, Eliot, Blunden. The Thirties showed a falling-off (perhaps because the main writers were already Fellows). The most distinguished of them would seem to be Rabindranath Tagore, but when he was recommended for the Academic Committee, Gosse wrote to say that the Lord Chancellor strongly disapproved of him being appointed, and that he himself (Gosse, that is) agreed that Tagore was an unsuitable candidate. No reason is given for their disapproval. Was it racism, or did something else come into it?

Then came the Second World War, and on thin, brownish wartime paper the 1945 list shows that Fellows were elected in the previous six years, but not many. By 1947 the literary world seemed alive again, and twenty Fellows of real worth, with Churchill leading off, were elected. In the half century since then, almost every writer of note has been involved with the RSL.

A PATINA of myth covers the origins of most organisations after a very short time. The story is told, re-told, and becomes set in anecdotal concrete. Legends, perhaps invented, are taken as history.

In the case of the RSL, the first of these myths concerns the date usually taken as that of its foundation. Most often this is given as 1823 or even 1825, the year in which it obtained its charter. *The Learned Societies and Printing Clubs of the United Kingdom*, published in 1847, already has the foundation date as 1823. The mistake was repeated over and over again, and although the earliest records clearly show the RSL up and running in 1820, the centenary banquet was held, with great pomp and the Earl of Balfour in the chair, on 20 November 1925, the centenary of the Royal Charter, not of the foundation itself.

But a handwritten, unsigned short history, dark with age and with its last pages missing, says: "The foundation of the Royal Society of Literature should date from the year of the Accession of George IV, for not only had the draft outline of its objects been with Royal assent printed and circulated in that year, but its first rough memo-book exists, with the Heading 'Royal Society of Literature', and there are recorded the proceedings of ten preliminary meetings, held at Messrs Hatchards, Piccadilly, between Nov. 30th 1820 and April 19th 1821." That this anonymous writer was correct in taking 1820 as the date of the RSL's foundation is confirmed by an article in the Literary Gazette of 16 December 1820, which gave a long account of the new Society. A fortnight later, on 1 January 1821, the *Repository of Arts, Literature, Fashions, Manufactures, &c* repeated its information, with a flowery preface, headed ROYAL SOCIETY OF LITERATURE. John Harford, biographer of the non-royal founder, also says: "It was founded in the year 1820, under the special patronage of his Majesty George IV."

Plenty of possibly not quite accurate tales (since they differ in detail and emphasis they cannot all be entirely accurate) have gathered around this foundation, but of its date there can be no doubt. It was shortly before the end of November 1820, the brain-child, though quite casually conceived, of Thomas Burgess, bishop of St David's and later of Salisbury. His own account, given in 1831, soon after the death of George IV, was probably the first formal one:

"The Government of this country had long been subject to the reproach of neglecting the general interest of learning and never had a prince succeeded to the Throne, since the days of Elizabeth, so initiated in the best principles of classical and general knowledge, and so endowed with congenial taste and talent, as His late Majesty; and therefore so well prepared to do away the national reproach. This impression gave rise to the suggestion of a plan for the advancement of learning by royal patronage, in a circle of private friends — a suggestion, therefore, apparently very far removed from the probability of reaching the royal ear.

George IV (1762-1830) as Prince Regent, an engraving owned by the Society. He was the Society's first royal patron

But the plan, thus casually suggested, was communicated, by one of the persons present, to a confidential servant of the King, and by him to His Majesty himself. An audience at Carlton House was almost the immediate consequence."

In this account, the king is given credit for inspiring, in a roundabout way, the idea of a literary society in "a circle of private friends". The "confidential servant" was almost certainly Sir Benjamin Bloomfield, the king's private secretary. But earlier, in 1823, in his address to the RSL at the first General Meeting, Burgess gives the king total credit for founding the RSL, and takes none of it himself. There is no mention of the original idea, of the group of friends told about it, of Bloomfield's intervention in relaying the idea to the king. "To His Majesty's love of learning, and desire to promote the Literature of His Country, the Society owes its existence," he says. "A general outline of a Society of Literature having been, by the command of the King, submitted to His Majesty, on the 2nd of November, 1820, it was His Majesty's pleasure, that a Society should be formed." There are further references to the king's munificence, "which cannot fail to have a powerful influence on the rising generation", to his "magnificent design for the advancement of Literature", to his "beneficent and patriotic views", and so on, but nothing about Burgess's crucial role in the foundation. Why? Was it because the king had to be deferred, indeed kowtowed, to in everything? Was it modesty? Was it flattery? It is hard to understand just what Burgess was trying to say or do with this fulsome, but it seems not strictly accurate, account of how the RSL began.

Another recorder of early events was William Jerdan, whose four-volume *Autobiography*, published in 1853, has a long chapter on the RSL, which he supported enthusiastically almost from the start, particularly in the *Literary Gazette*, of which he was editor. In its earliest stage James Christie, second in the line of auctioneers, told him about it. "The institution is a favourite plan of his Majesty," Christie wrote, "who has engaged the Bishop of St David's to form it and to enrol the first members." The suggestion here is that the king was the creative force, the bishop merely his executor. If it was really George IV who first had the idea of the Society, and Burgess who carried out his plan, then the bishop's 1831 account of its origins in "a circle of private friends" cannot have been true; but no-one seems ever to have suggested that Yet Burgess's biographer, Harford, an ardent admirer of his subject, gives a similar account of the Society's origins: "George IV... summoned the Bishop of St David's to his presence, soon after his accession to the throne, and committed, in a most flattering manner, to his judgement the task of framing the plan of a society for the advancement of these objects."

Harford was so passionately concerned to show Bishop Burgess in the best possible light that it seems odd he denied him credit for thinking up the idea of the RSL. Did he feel it was more to Burgess's credit that the king should seek him out, from among all his subjects, to put into effect a plan of his own, rather than that the Bishop should first have thought up the plan and explained it to the king? Impossible to tell. In the 558 pages of his biography of Burgess, Harford gives only four pages to the RSL proper, so perhaps he elided the early events, concentrating them into a couple of sentences, and thus altering the way in which Burgess said things had happened. Harford's book was published in 1840, ten years after Burgess's account and twenty after the founding of the RSL, so myths had had time to proliferate and memories to fade.

It is hard to believe that the idea of the RSL was originally the king's because, if it had been, it seems unlikely he would have picked Burgess to carry it out. George IV had plenty of friends better qualified to set up a literary society, and (one would imagine) more congenial to himself. Two men more unalike it would be hard to find, and, apart from their temperamental differences, Burgess was an odd choice for the task. Although he published over a hundred works he was not what we would now call a literary man: today he would hardly be eligible as a Fellow, let alone be thought qualified to be the Society's leader and the moulder of its first seventy-five years. He always maintained that the RSL's objects were "to reward literary merit, and to excite literary talent". But what did he mean by literary? Nothing in his own works could be given such a label. These were either theological, biblical, sociological, linguistic, didactic, classical, or polemical. All his publications can be slotted into one or other of these categories.

In other words, he was a divine rather than a man of letters or a writer. His best remembered achievement was the establishment, not of the RSL, but of a college for clerical

Thomas Burgess (1756-1837) Bishop of St David's, and later Bishop of Salisbury, the first President of the Royal Society of Literature

education at Lampeter, St David's, now part of the University of Wales. He was wholly taken up with theological matters and his duties as a churchman, and even when he touched upon something literary, it was only to dig out its theological meaning and purpose. On literature he held prescriptive views which the king (a liberal, as well as a libertine, at least in his youth, which people tend to forget) would surely not have approved. In his first address to the RSL Burgess spoke of "the connexion, which the cultivation of the higher branches of Literature has with everything that is morally good in society"; elsewhere he banished Gibbon from the canon of approved writers on moral grounds, and would surely have banned Byron and Shelley on the same grounds. A bigot, narrow in his views and interests, prim in the Victorian manner before the reign of Victoria, he seems the last person likely to be liked by the raffish monarch.

On slavery he took the liberal line; on Roman Catholicism, for which he had a rabid hatred, he seems scarcely sane. Since Wellington was the villain of 1829 (for supporting the Catholic Emancipation bill), Burgess was often heard to say, gloomily and illogically, "We owe all this to the battle of Waterloo."

After Harford's biography of Burgess came a fifty-year gap in the telling of the tale, until in the 1890s Sir Edward Brabrook's short *History of the Royal Society of Literature* appeared. It began with the long-accepted version of the RSL's foundation ("In October 1820, in 'accidental conversation', a person who can be identified as Thomas Burgess..."), and much of it is an account of who died in what year, with complete obituaries. The long one on Coleridge, eight and a half pages of small print, by the then president of the Society, the Earl of Ripon, fails to mention "Kubla Khan", "Christabel", "The Rime of the Ancient Mariner" or "Frost at Midnight". Brabrook has long lists of activists, prize winners and medallists, presidents and vice-presidents, royal dukes and clerics, council members and council meetings: not an exciting read, but all we have from that time.

In the year mysteriously considered the Society's centenary, 1925, the then president, the Marquis of Crewe, gave a paper on its history to celebrate the mistakenly-dated event. He followed Brabrook in giving the early facts, but emphasised rather more the chancy nature of the Society's royal foundation. "It was in 1820, Sir Edward tells us, that Burgess, the Bishop of St David's, casually mentioned the 'advantages which might be expected from the institution of a Society of Literature somewhat resembling the French Academy of Belles Lettres' ...The Royal Society of Literature does not seem to have developed from the friendly symposia of a few enthusiasts, but to have sprung, so to speak, all armed from the episcopal brain."

Twenty years later, an American called David Williams wrote a PhD thesis on *The Royal Society of Literature and the patronage of George IV*, published in 1945 in Cambridge, Massachusetts, as one of the Harvard dissertations in American and English literature. It is long — 114 pages of preface and introduction, 432 pages of text, 268 of notes, index, lists of dedications to the king and so on — detailed, verbose and rather heavily written; but useful, full of information about most aspects of the RSL in its earliest stages and those involved with it. In detail its story goes up to 1831, just after the death of George IV, with brief final chapters on the subsequent history of the Society.

I will end the tale of the RSL's earliest days with one of those jokey anecdotes which become embedded in early histories and are then, for ever after, impossible either to dislodge or to be sure about. It was said (some believed it, some did not) that the king intended to give the new Society 1000 guineas as a one-off payment. Instead, Burgess believed he meant to give 1000 guineas *annually*, and went about telling everyone (including the public prints) how splendidly generous this was. Wryly, when he was told that everyone expected it, the king threw up his hands and agreed to pay up annually. To look mean when he was praised for being lavish would have been impossible, and, as Lord Crewe put it, "parsimony was not one of his vices".

But was it really so? As with much else in those early days, it is impossible to know. Was it an innocent misunderstanding? Or was Burgess wilier than one knows, and did he lay a trap for a patron he knew was genial, careless with money and openhanded?

T HEY TOILED hard over the preliminary papers which would set up the RSL — the prospectuses, the arrangements for awards and associates, the reports and finally the Charter of Incorporation, which would give it a permanent status. Everything was scrutinised and much changed, with papers in the end looking like palimpsests. All these had to be approved by the king, and he duly approved them. How carefully he examined them we cannot tell, but Burgess assured everyone of his close attention and enthusiastic support and Brabrook in his history suggested he had had a good deal to do with the early drafts. It was mainly Burgess and Jerdan who did the preliminary work; and Jerdan who, as editor of the *Literary Gazette*, had a forum from which to spread the news. A few other literary reviews copied his, and some (Macaulay the most famous — and the most amusing — of these) responded with ferocious criticism before the Society was even on its feet.

It was not particularly significant that the first committee meeting (at Hatchards) took place on 30 November 1820, the day after Queen Caroline went in state to St Paul's Cathedral to celebrate the abandonment of the Bill of Pains and Penalties two weeks before. But royal rows were as much part of the history of the times as they are today and the royal founder of the RSL inevitably raised the hackles of those who supported the queen, and made them believe in the political rather than the purely literary point of the new Society. From the first the disaffected believed it was a creature of the Tories, therefore to be hated and harassed by the Whigs — indeed by all libertarians, republicans, dissidents and non-joiners — and treated, however hard it tried not to be, as politically biased.

The king was anxious for it to be non-party, and seen to be so. A careful look at the credentials of those who joined makes it clear that all parties and factions were represented, but however hard its non-political status was stressed a feeling often remained that "loyalty" to the crown — a much-used word — was part of its ethos. Queen Caroline's supporters must therefore dislike and despise it and the king's friends must support it. That was about as far as politics went, but on a broader basis the attitudes of Burgess and others like him must have put off anyone who disliked being preached to in matters of morals.

In the *Literary Gazette* Jerdan was at best tactless, at worst infuriating: he wrote of "turning the genius of England into the current of English loyalty", and added: "We are full of the conviction that this measure [the foundation of the RSL] will be the source of a renovated vigour in constitutional loyalty." Loyalty to the crown, that is.

In his vision of the future to be opened up by the RSL Jerdan became not just rhetorical but almost ecstatic and again the emphasis is on royal munificence and royal patronage: "What intellectual influx may come when the royal liberality pauses in its orbit above 'that tide divine', and shoots down its ray direct!" Jerdan then went on to the attack. Poets "on the disaffected side", he wrote, "have, to the disgust of all good men, and the disgrace of their art, levelled their chief attacks at the individual to whom duty and feeling should have offered their first homage" (that is, the king). As Williams remarked: "If it is the society's hope to avoid partisan politics, the *Literary Gazette* is surely starting off on the wrong foot." Controversy continued, in spite of the king's hope for a non-partisan Society; whipped up (again, as happens today) by the press.

The Society, the first draft of the prospectus said, was to consist of Honorary Members, Subscribing Members, and Associates. By 1821, subscribing Members had become Fellows, three of whom were needed to propose anyone for election. Then, after protests from the Royal Academy and the Royal Society that FRSL would be too close to *their* designation of Fellows, Fellows became Members again. The question of who is called what in the RSL has a byzantine complexity, with frequent changes down the years. Honorary Members comprised "some of the most eminent men in the Three Kingdoms and the most distinguished female writers". (The question of female writers pops up again at the end of the nineteenth century when women, after much discussion and some opposition, were allowed to be elected as Fellows. There were, as far as I can discover, three women members in the Society's earliest days, but these appear to have been forgotten later in the nineteenth century, when the RSL was very much a male social club.)

What are today called members, which means anyone who likes to join, were allowed in from 1918. This has made an enormous difference to the Society's life and atmosphere, as women Fellows also have. (Of them, I need not write — the effects of women's admission are obvious.) People with literary interests, not necessarily professional writers, have greatly enlarged the Society's range, increasing its numbers at lectures, opening windows on to a wider world than that of the Fellows, which may sometimes appear hermetic, and helping to keep the Society financially afloat by paying the same subscription as the Fellows.

Associates were to be "Twenty men of distinguished learning, Authors of some creditable Work of Literature, and men of good moral character; Ten under the Patronage of the king, and Ten under the Patronage of the Society". Each Associate must give a dissertation every year (this rule was soon dropped as there were too many Associates for the time available). Meetings were to be held weekly from February to July; monthly in the rest of the year.

The general aims of the RSL were "to unite and extend the general interest of literature; to reward literary merit by patronage; to excite literary talent by premiums; and to promote literary education". Details of subscription charges and times of meetings seem absurd in these broad pre-liminary statements. Had no one thought, for instance, that money values might change and particular charges become obsolete? Or that lifestyles might change, and office work might make meetings at 2pm difficult for many? Presum-ably not.

Things nearly shuddered to a halt, to the confusion and dismay of the founders, when Sir Walter Scott denounced the idea of an RSL and it was thought the king might listen to him and withdraw his favour. Scott had then so much literary influence — so much personal influence with the king, as well — that it was hardly surprising for Burgess,

Jerdan and the other fairly small fry to feel they were facing a crisis. Arguments batted back and forth in the press between Jerdan and his opponents were one thing. Scott's was heavyweight opposition. In a long letter to John Charles Villiers, who in 1824 became the third Earl of Clarendon, and was present at the first small meeting which discussed the RSL in 1820, he set out his case against the new Society.

It was one repeated in all the attacks on the Society, then and later: booksellers and the reading public supported writers far more generously than the proposed RSL pensions would, and private patronage was anyway preferable; brilliant writers like Byron would be excluded for political reasons (and Burgess's views, on narrowly moral grounds, would have kept them out as well); mediocre men and "university pedants" would be attracted to membership and prizes; it would be impossible to set standards of criticism; the English hated being lectured on matters of taste; private patronage would be discouraged; the stigma of charity would deter some and humiliate others; the lowest common denominator would rule; and, inevitably, there would be quarrels and factions. And so on and so on. Villiers showed the letter to Lord Sidmouth, and the pair of them probably showed it to the king; and, according to Jerdan, the founders were "staggered". For a time all seemed lost.

Then, as so often happened in the days of personal influence rather than official rules, something chancy turned the tide. Prince Hoare, playwright, art historian and in Jerdan's words "one of the most zealous and effective members of the Committee" (he had been involved in the formation and drafting of the constitution), happened to live in Brighton. So, at that moment, in his Pavilion, did the king. And somehow, through the efforts of the king's chaplain and the wife of his chamberlain, Hoare managed, "over wine and walnuts", to put the RSL's case to the king, who said in effect "Carry on". The king, it seems, took no notice of Scott's objections and believed that "where he did not lead he was not much inclined to co-operate, and far less to follow".

Greatly relieved, the committee went back to its plans and within a month Scott seemed, after all, to have accepted the inevitability of the RSL. Later, he was to accept a gold medal from it as well, so his opposition cannot have been as fiery as his letter suggested. Apart from small digs like calling Cattermole, the Secretary, Catterwaul, he even became quite friendly. Southey, also originally critical, later came round to the RSL as well.

Leigh Hunt attacked the new Society in *The Examiner*; but the wittiest attack of all, far more effective than Scott's prosy letter or the chippy pieces by journalists, came from the young Macaulay. A Star Chamber of the Muses, he said, would be full of envy, factions and political bias: "Whigs would canvas against a Southey, Tories against a Byron." The essay repays reading for its gusto and punch, though to my mind it tails off at the end when it brings in an over-long jokey comparison between the RSL and a wine society.

Those early years saw depressingly slow progress in the advance of the RSL. This was especially noticeable when it

The Report includes an address by the Provisional President, Bishop Burgess, which sets out the 'origin of the Society'

REPORT

OF THE

PROCEEDINGS

OF

The Royal Society of Literature,

AT ITS

FIRST GENERAL MEETING,

On TUESDAY, THE 17th Day of JUNE, 1823.

(Printed by Order of the Council.)

———◆———

THE first *General Meeting* of the ROYAL SOCIETY OF LITERATURE, convened by public Advertisement, and by a Circular, stating the business with which the Meeting would be chiefly occupied, (both issued under the authority of the *Provisional Council,*) was holden on Tuesday, June 17th, at the House of the Literary Fund Society, in Lincoln's Inn Fields.

At Half-past Two o'Clock the Chair was taken by THE BISHOP OF ST. DAVID'S, *Provisional President* of the Society.

was compared with other societies set up at about the same time and quickly successful. The Royal Asiatic Society and its offshoot the Oriental Translation Committee, and the Royal Academy of Music (where Dickens's sister Fanny was one of its first pupils, aged twelve), became instantly respected and influential. What Williams called the RSL's "slow convolutions" were mortifying. In 1823 its constitution and regulations were published in quarto volumes; in 1824, the prospectus and by-laws. The ten Royal Associates were chosen. Prizes set up for anonymous entrants were soon withdrawn, entries returned as unworthy. Instead annual medals were given without competition. Southey and Campbell refused to be Royal Associates because of the money attached: Southey liking the honour but not the pension, and Campbell being unwilling to be "bought".

Members tended to be old: two thirds over fifty, a third over sixty, a sixth over seventy; this at a time when a man was thought elderly at fifty. When the Reverend C.A. Heurtley died in 1937 he had been a member for sixty-nine years. No wonder Scott called them "the Gaffers or Gammers of Literature". "Sound morals and religion [were] requirements for any participation in the privileges of the Society," Burgess said in his annual address. At another he tried to prove that the Apostle Paul had visited Britain and preached; and rode his hobby horse, Milton's theology as expressed in *De Natura Christiana*, a recently discovered treatise on the Trinity. Council and officers included one marquis (who became a duke), one viscount (who became an earl), one baron, two baronets, two knights, two further

MPs (one of whom became an earl, the other a baron), two bishops, two archdeacons, six lesser clergymen, and a colonel.

Everything was not unliterary or undistinguished, though. Among the first members were some interesting names, as well as refusals. Canning, for instance, was asked by Jerdan to join but replied that he "had early determined to have nothing to do with it"; though later, three months before his death in 1827, he did in fact join (perhaps he had found the pushy Jerdan uncongenial). In the first list of members were two more bishops; the Lord Chief Justice who in 1827 became Lord Tenterden; Sir Thomas Lawrence, the most famous portrait painter of the day and President of the Royal Academy; two leading headmasters, John Russell of Charterhouse (from Thackeray's time there) and Samuel Butler of Shrewsbury, grandfather of his namesake who wrote *Erewhon* and that great novel *The Way of All Flesh*; William Wilberforce, the great reformer; Francis Chantrey the sculptor; William Hamilton, Lord Elgin's secretary, a keen collector like his namesake, Emma's husband, who recovered the Elgin marbles from the sea-bed (W.M. Leake, classical topographer, numismatist and RSL vice president, lost all his recent manuscripts on an Egyptian survey in the same shipwreck, but, unlike the marbles, they could not be rescued); the future Lord Dover, who was president of the Society; Lord Lansdowne, another future president; Lord Morpeth, later the Earl of Carlisle; Henry Hallam the historian, winner of the RSL's gold medal, father of Tennyson's *In Memoriam* friend Arthur Hallam; John Landseer, painter, engraver, writer, and father of the more famous

Edwin; Isaac Goldsmid, the first Jewish baronet, who worked for the emancipation of his people and was the activist behind the Jewish Disabilities Act in 1854, the year of his death; William Ayrton, who introduced Italian opera to London; Byron's publisher John Murray; John Bell, publisher and bookseller, who was the main distributor of French books in England and the first to introduce a lower-case s to match its next-door fellow instead of the long f-like letter (the practice continued in handwriting for many years: as a child I had several letters addressed to me as Mifs); and Sith Beg, dragoman to the Prince of Persia, to add some exotic colour.

And of course there was Coleridge. With Robert Malthus, who was hardly literary but whose work was, and remains, important, he was one of the two Royal Associates whose fame has lasted, and who seems worthy of the honour, though meagrely rewarded with his hundred yearly guineas (which nonetheless he needed badly, and missed when they were withdrawn). Scott might sneer that it was only what an upper servant was paid in a grand household, but to someone as poor as Coleridge it meant a great deal. And it is his name that shines most brightly at the founding of the RSL. Anyone who now asks what writers belonged to it at its start, and who was a Royal Associate, is immediately startled and impressed to hear Coleridge's name. Not that he was a particularly eager or active participant; but at once he adds lustre to the Society's history.

And he gave me my moment of purest excitement, keenest joy. In drawers and files and all sorts of unexpected crannies there were letters and cards and other writings in their own hand from Crabbe, Southey, Malthus and Decimus Burton, Yeats and Shaw, Beerbohm and Forster, Wells and Wodehouse, Barrie, David Jones, Auden and Beckett; and mixed up with a pile of cheque-stubs was a letter in Edmund Blunden's unmistakable handwriting. But who would expect to find, in a modern envelope, four documents (three receipts and the synopsis of a lecture) written by Coleridge, papers never seen by scholarly researchers, unheard of (I am assured) on the academic circuit?

1825 came, and with it the Charter of Incorporation. The Society was now established, its future assured.

FOUNDERS

GEORGE IV has been vilified so heartily that it is hard to consider him coolly as founder of the RSL, or at least its promoter and patron. "A creature lazy, weak, indolent, of monstrous vanity and levity incurable" seems to have been, and still seems to be, a widespread view of him. "A libertine over head and ears in debt... without a single claim on the gratitude of his country or the respect of posterity" was Leigh Hunt's opinion of him; "that royal old mummy" was Thackeray's. Herbert Spencer set him among "the criminal classes", Beddoes consigned him to "a warmer climate than India", and others compared him with figures as diverse as Prince Hal, Richard III, Falstaff, Othello and Henry VIII. His vast girth in middle age was a gift to cartoonists and an excuse for mockery by everyone; even Scott, whom he admired so much, referred to him (not unaffectionately, perhaps) as "our fat friend".

It was Gilray and Rowlandson's age of brilliant caricature and cruel exaggeration. But there were kinder views of George IV, not confined to the sycophantic early members of the RSL (among them the highminded Bishop Burgess), who used the conventionally extravagant language (which can be discounted) of courtiers and those seeking or acknowledging patronage. More sensible men sometimes praised him, not to his face and absurdly, but behind his back and soberly. John Murray told Scott that when the prince (as he then was) met Byron, he "displayed an intim-

[41]

acy and critical taste which at once surprised and delighted [him]"; Dr Charles Burney wrote to his daughter Fanny: "I was astonished to find him, amidst so much dissipation, possessed of so much learning, wit, knowledge of books in general, discrimination of character, as well as original humour." Many others found him likeable; from this distance he often seems so.

From the RSL's point of view, it is his patronage of literature that counts. Clearly he wanted to support literature in general as well as individual writers. He cared about books, liked the company of writers, sought them out, enjoyed meeting them and forwarding their careers, even spotting their talents. As far as his position allowed, he was a friend of Sheridan and Scott; he arranged government appointments or sinecures for Thomas Moore, Sheridan and others; helped Crabbe, met Horace Walpole and Lord Chesterfield, both elderly, and, most significantly, had the wit to recognise the genius of Jane Austen long before she was widely known or appreciated. He admired Scott enormously, offered to make him a privy councillor and made him the first baronet of his reign — indeed, the first literary baronet; he appointed Southey poet laureate, gave financial help to indigent writers through the Literary Fund Society (now the Royal Literary Fund) and to theatres, dramatists, actors and singers, contributed to the setting up of monuments to Shakespeare and Burns, supported literary causes, reviews and the important Oriental Translation Committee, and gave his father's library of 65,000 volumes to the nation.

By founding the RSL he committed himself for the rest of his life to giving yearly pensions of a hundred guineas to ten Royal Associates, two gold medals worth fifty guineas each, and land for an RSL house in central London. This, it has been said, was meagre in comparison with what he spent on buildings and works of art, but in comparison with what sovereigns before and after him gave to literature it was lavish. As soon as he died his brother William IV withdrew payment of the pensions, and, I have come to suspect, possibly the promised building plot as well. By comparison with the reign that came after his, George IV's short bountiful one was something of a golden, or at least a silver, age for the world of letters.

A mezzotint of a lost portrait of George IV hung in the main room downstairs at Hyde Park Gardens. It shows the King as youngish, clean-shaven, with his own hair, which is thick and curly, and a kindly, pleasant expression: it looks a "good" face. In comparison with the whiskery Victorians who came after him, he looks modern, and he certainly seems so in comparison with Bishop Burgess who, in a curious white wig rather like a crash helmet, with plate-like swathes over each ear, seems very much from another century, as well as another world.

A portrait of Burgess hung upstairs. His clothes are sumptuous, an amazing array of velvet, ribbons, bows, cords and cascades of lawn, many yards of which must have been needed to make the enormous sleeves of his outfit. He wears small ovoid spectacles and sits on a curlicued chair, with knobs and cherubs carved behind the wig. Face and wig are recognisable in a small statue also owned by the RSL, possibly the maquette for a larger statue, kept under a glass dome. In it he sits in flowing clerical robes

[43]

and buckled shoes, writing on what looks like a rather wobbly knee, head down, a greyish-white clay figure about a foot high.

This was the man who gathered the earliest members of the Society around him. They do not sound an inspiring lot, and to brighter sparks seemed mediocre, perpetuating their own dowdiness by choosing others like themselves. Most were not what we would call men of letters. Of the twenty members of the first Council, six were bishops, two archdeacons, two tutors to the royal children — a singularly ill-educated lot, by the sound of it — one was a physician to the Prince of Wales, and one a Keeper of Antiquities at the British Museum. Others connected with the setting up of the RSL were the Chancellor of the Exchequer; a high sheriff of Essex; a man who had reconstructed the government of Ceylon; James Christie, of the auctioneering family; a friend of Burgess's rather oddly commended for his "high respectability in trade"; and, as far as I can discover the only specifically literary one, the Keeper of Printed Books at the British Museum.

It was a downward spiral throughout most of the nineteenth century. By 1894, just before the RSL's spectacular turnabout and improvement, the standard of papers given in the *Transactions*, which were supposed to cream off the very best, could publish such gibberish as this: "The ever-widening stream of English poetry had, in the time of Elizabeth, become a majestic flood, flowing deeply and tunefully amid the flowery meads of song. By the banks of this stately river there then existed, and still exist, unfrequented paths leading to secluded retreats, hidden by the shade of verdant foliage, sweet with the breath of wild-flowers, and where wimpling streamlets, fed from the parent source, made their own low, sweet music amid scenes of ever-varying beauty, sacred to Nature and her perennial charms. Here the crooning brooklets sang amid the amorous sunshine, making the verdure gay and the flowers rejoice; and here the devastating hand of Time has still spared the sequestered dells of delight, in which is still preserved much of that English song-bloom, whose fragrance still is wafted into the hearts of those who dwell within our island home. To one of those little-known but beautiful song-haunts I wish to conduct you this afternoon."

No wonder the great Victorians steered clear.

CHANGES

THE IDEA of the RSL as an Academy had been in the air from the start. One of the first long statements of intent, setting out its plans and objectives, is in fact headed Royal *Academy* of Literature. In his history Brabrook mentions Burgess's belief in "a Society of Literature, somewhat resembling the French Academy of Belles Lettres"; and others down the years have said the same sort of thing. But in the 1820s the word Academy, and with it the idea it suggests, was soon dropped. (Come to that, so was the idea of, though not the word, "literature".) In the first public statement — the one sent out from Hatchards, announcing prizes in 1820 — the body was called what it was to remain, the Royal Society of Literature.

Thoughts of an Academy lingered, however; the wish for something more decisive and didactic (more strict and bossy, some might say), with more intellectual effect, more power to influence education, learning, the universities, culture and the world in general, something which would sweep into every corner of rational, moral and imaginative life. Today, the notion would probably raise smiles, and be called elitist; but the word was not used then, and if it had been would have had no pejorative meaning. The best was unarguably the best, great minds were indisputably the greatest. But why did the idea of an Academy, an arbiter in the use of the language, a propagandist for English and its literature, quite suddenly come to the RSL, a comet in a quiet sky, in 1909?

[47]

For many reasons, large and small. The RSL's story cannot be seen in a vacuum. Great events and national moods shaped it, as they always shape people's lives. In 1820, things were very different. As Jerdan put it: "Riots and disturbances, and affairs of threatening political aspect, kept the public in a ferment, and distracted the government." The French Revolution was within living memory, its terrors and hopes still vivid. Every riot and disturbance suggested that similar horrors might be on the way in Britain. In 1909, though, the next upheavals of the western world — the First World War and the Russian Revolution — were still to come. Those years before them seem, in retrospect at least, a time of stability for the educated few within the RSL ambit, cushioned against disaster; the time before everything fell apart. Even the weather, memoirs and fiction suggest, was for a few years golden.

Britain was riding high in confidence, in a belief in its own power and influence (for good, of course that meant) wherever the map was coloured pink. The Empire on which the sun never set — the idea of Empire — pervaded every aspect of English life, particularly dreams of the future, of personal fulfilment. So when the idea of an Academy was pulled out again, after ninety somnolent years, it seemed clearly part of a larger plan. England was seen not as isolated, tucked away in a north-western corner of Europe, but as the centre of a world-wide association of peoples to whom the English language and its literature were culturally paramount.

Everything that happened in the RSL has to be seen with this in mind. The mood was one of sanguine anticipation, high hopes, far-fetched ambitions. Anything could happen, and things that might now seem absurdly impractical then appeared possible. The RSL Council at that time was composed mainly of administrators, useful packhorses rather than impressive writers. It was the impressive writers who called in others like themselves to set up what was later called, openly in a report, an *"imperium in imperio"*. Few in the general membership (which in 1909 meant elected Fellows) seemed to query its existence or its rights.

It happened quite suddenly. "The Academic Committee of the RSL came into existence in May 1910," a report says later. "No such body was contemplated in the Charter of the Society; and it was formed merely by a resolution passed at the General Anniversary Meeting of 1910." But we must go back a little, to the Council meeting of 8 December 1909, when it was said that "the powers conferred upon the Royal Society of Literature of the United Kingdom, by its Royal Charter of 1825, include many of the most useful objects of an Academy of Letters." "Its composition and resources," the minutes went on, "warrant the belief that arrangements might be made which would enable the Society effectively to attain them... and that a committee be appointed to consider the foregoing." The suggestion was carried unanimously. If the Council was cutting its own throat no-one seemed to notice.

By May, fourteen distinguished writers, who had not joined the RSL until then, were elected Honorary Fellows so that they could become part of what was then called, and continued to be called, the Academic Committee of English Letters. According to Charles Pulley, Secretary to the RSL just before the Second World War, Edmund Gosse was its main instigator. Certainly his letters show that he wanted to make it clear that the Academic Committee and the RSL were entirely separate bodies. Although the Council minutes make it seem sudden, things had been going on behind the scenes for some time. Those who thought up the idea of an Academic Committee went to the Society of Authors for advice, and the two chose the Academic Committee members together. Those who suspected the committee would break away from the RSL and seek a new charter were told that the new body was simply carrying out the wishes of the old charter of 1825. The appointment of twenty Royal Associates in the early years had been the same sort of thing (it was said). Ten were pensioned by the king, ten simply honoured, but all were thought to contribute to the prestige of the Society, as indeed these new ones were to do in 1910, much more successfully than the first group. Nearly all the early Associates were soon forgotten (with the exception of Coleridge and Malthus, they were pretty forgettable). The new ones were not. All the same, the Academic Committee provoked rumbles of dissent among members and criticism in the press. It was thought unfair to the general membership, and certainly undemocratic, to have an unelected, handpicked team. Brabrook tried to bring the two sides together by putting Shaw and Lady Ritchie (Thackeray's daughter) on the Council as well as on their own new committee.

From the minute book of the Academic Committee

First Meeting Tuesday 19th July 1910   3 p.m.

Edmund Gosse
Lawrence Binyon
W B Yeats
Austin Dobson

Henry Newbolt
E. H. Pember
S. H. Butcher
A. C. Lyall

On the suggestion of Mr Gosse, cordially received,
Mr S. H. Butcher took the Chair.

1. Letters were read from the Presidents of the British
Academy & the Royal Society, expressing
thanks for the invitations to nominate Representatives of those societies on the Academic
Committee, & cordial good wishes to
the Royal Society of Literature, but stating a
disinclination to accede.

To those within it, this was known as the AC, and for the next two decades it dominated the Society. No doubt its work was done by a few, as happens in most committees, but its membership was large (officially up to forty) and impressive. It meant that almost every notable writer at the time was involved in its doings and that the glory of these names rubbed off on the RSL in general. This was recognised by its organisers: a memo suggests that if famous writers are asked to join the Academic Committee they are more likely to accept than if they are invited to go on the Council and see to the routine chores.

For some years the AC seems to have been almost autonomous. It had its own paper for memos and letters, with ACADEMIC COMMITTEE printed large and the RSL acknowledged in much smaller type. It had its own bank account at Coutts, started by A.C. Benson with £100. Apart from the day-to-day running of the Society, it seems to have taken over most of the RSL's literary functions, with frequent meetings and talks. It chose both subjects and speakers. In the days before photocopiers and other office aids it must have created a vast amount of work in its small headquarters. The AC secretary, Mrs Margaret Woods, a very likeable-sounding woman, tireless and cheerful despite all sorts of ailments, wrote nearly all the letters in longhand. The committee met every month and, despite Gosse's disapproval ("I am wholly against providing tea. It is pure waste and confusion"), had tea. The packhorses continued to carry some of the work on the Council (some AC members, as I have said, were Council members as well). Technically the Council was still in charge and supposed to vet what the AC was up to; but its members were now less influential in the Society's affairs.

Before me, in his neat legible hand, I have two copies of Gosse's list of hopes and plans: "The aims of an Academy of Letters founded on the scheme of the Académie française would be, to protect the English language against all attempts to reduce it to vulgarity, and to hold up a standard of purity and good taste in style. To encourage fellowship between those who are disinterestedly striving for the perfection of English literature. By 'discourses of reception' and by obituary addresses to mark the current of literary history in the country. To help in the production of such inedited works of interest and value as may from time to time be discovered or become accessible. To issue medals and prizes in recognition of separate works of remarkable merit by new writers. To issue an occasional prize, or medal, as a recompense for the entire work of an eminent man. To administer, or advise, in the administration [of] charitable funds."

Of these schemes the first, which seemed central and gave the AC its name, was in the long term the least successful. The rest were easy to cope with: fellowship among writers, prizes, medals and honours, obituaries and addresses of welcome to new Fellows. The AC met to discuss all kinds of things (Shaw wanted poets to read their own work, for instance), to give awards, publicise literary matters, give literary advice (to the prime minister about the duties of the poet laureate, for instance), and, perhaps most strikingly, to impress the world with its collective voice and imposing membership. A letter signed by a dozen writers

[53]

known to the public was obviously going to have more effect than one signed by a dozen unknown Council members, however hard-working and devoted to the RSL.

Much harder to implement than the easy schemes was the very idea of an Academy of Letters. What really was its function? What could it hope to achieve or even influence? Were its aims impossibly ambitious? Those it tried to implement were small-scale, on the fringes of larger schemes. There was a plan to set up a phonetic alphabet, so that foreigners would find it easier to pronounce English correctly, and the native English (the uneducated, that is) would improve their pronunciation (shades of Professor Higgins). An amusing but seriously intentioned questionnaire went round asking members of the AC exactly how they pronounced certain words (an early example of U and Non-U). Did they say *lahndry* or *laundry*, for instance?

Even in 1910 the range of spoken English was enormous, the possibility of enforcing rules about it minute. Today, the idea of an Academy on French lines seems so improbable that it is not seriously considered, and seldom even discussed. English is now admitted to be the world language — used in commerce, banking, air travel, in far-flung places everywhere, even in diplomacy, where French was so long dominant. But what kind of English, in what kind of situation? How close are these varied versions to "received" English, the central, supposedly accentless kind spoken by the educated, at one time heard in broadcasting so universally that it was known as BBC English? Today it is heard more than anywhere on the BBC's World Service, as the version of English most intelligible to most people, particularly foreigners. Every other brand of English used to be judged against it, every divergence from it thought incorrect.

Today, things are so different that I need not spend space on describing (to literary readers in particular) why it is no longer monolithic and subject to regulation (except very simply and briefly: the language has become too widespread, too fluid and fast-changing, too split and scattered among national, racial and cultural groups; television penetrates everything; America, not Britain, is now the great world power and American, not English, English is the world language... and so on). But in 1910 and even some years later, it was still seriously thought that a tiny committee of academics in London could put its fist in the dyke and save the language from pollution around the world. Robert Bridges' Society for Pure English went even further, causing subsequent rows with the RSL, where nothing effective seems to have been done. Perhaps the AC knew in its heart that nothing could be done.

Whatever the final tally of its achievements, a dazzling array of writers joined the Academic Committee, either then or later, for long or short stays, actively or dozily. They included Joseph Conrad, Thomas Hardy, Henry James, W.B.Yeats, Laurence Binyon, Austin Dobson, G.M. Trevelyan, Robert Bridges, George Bernard Shaw, Arthur Pinero, Gilbert Murray, Edmund Blunden, A.C. Bradley, Harley Granville-Barker, A.W. Verrall, Lord Haldane, Edmund Gosse, James Frazer, Henry Newbolt, May Sinclair, J.W. Mackail, G.K. Chesterton, Arthur Conan Doyle, Arthur Quiller Couch, A.E.W. Mason, George Saintsbury, John

Drinkwater, A.C. Benson, Andrew Lang, Walter de la Mare, Walter Raleigh, John Morley, Maurice Hewlett, Lady Ritchie, Alfred Austin, Maurice Baring, T.S. Eliot, John Galsworthy, John Masefield, Siegfried Sassoon, Charles Morgan, Dean Inge, Max Beerbohm, H.A.L. Fisher, T. Sturge Moore and William de Morgan (who recalls the fact that artists belonged to the RSL in its early days, though he was also a novelist). And there were lesser fry (or fry who have since fallen out of favour), and no doubt others who have slipped down the cracks of the archives.

A few who were invited refused membership of the AC: A.E. Housman because it was "remote from [his] tastes and pursuits", Harold Nicolson and Vita Sackville-West courteously declining because they were too busy and too far from London, Virginia Woolf because, as a publisher, she felt she could not join a committee which would be giving prizes for books (the AC secretary wrote that she had written a "rational" letter, as if this was a cause for surprise). H.G. Wells told Gosse that he was "bitterly, incurably, destructively against Literary Academies". But on the whole people seemed pleased to be asked to join, perhaps lured at least a little by the eminence of everyone else: as the memo suggested, an invitation to join a highpowered

Members of the Academic Committee as seen by Max Beerbohm.
Clockwise from top left:
George Bernard Shaw, Walter Raleigh, Henry James, Edmund Gosse,
Laurence Binyon, Rudyard Kipling, Henry Newbolt, T. Sturge Moore,
W.B. Yeats, John Galsworthy, Arthur Wing Pinero, Anthony Hope,
J.M. Barrie, R.B. Haldane, Maurice Hewlett, John Morley,
Frederic Harrison, Thomas Hardy, Austin Dobson

committee was flattering, and the Council as it was then held no such lures.

Prize-giving, rather than wider linguistic matters, took up much of the AC's energy and time: looking out for suitable books, reading them, reporting on them, arguing about them, with the usual ups and downs which awards tend to produce. There are hints of sleaze, if not quite of scandal: a committee member tries to nobble Mrs Woods, to her indignation and dismay, over one of the awards; a near-winner is suddenly banned because of something else he has written (we are not told what, but it shakes the AC and Mrs Woods). But generally things go smoothly, and Miss Rudston Brown, the Secretary, makes suggestions from her bedtime reading.

Throughout the 1930s the AC was moribund, and hardly met at all; and the outbreak of war in 1939 finally put paid to it. Its founder-members, the original enthusiasts, were elderly, uninterested or dead, and its only function had become the adjudication of the Benson medals. Even this was done, on the last two occasions, through the post. An attempt was made to revive the ailing group by electing younger members, but nothing came of it, and it was decided to have the Benson medals considered by a committee of vice-presidents and Council members. In order to comply with the terms of the Benson bequest this would still have to be called — though it would keep changing its membership and be appointed only when needed — the Academic Committee.

So what had begun with fanfares was, in Charles Pulley's words, "peacefully dissolved". An unsigned memo early in 1939 sounds a sour note. "It would have been supposed," it says, "that if such a body as the AC existed, it would include the leading members of the RSL. But the President, eight of the ten Vice-Presidents and fourteen out of the fifteen members of the Council are not to be found on its roll. This ... consisted of nineteen members, of whom about half seldom or never take any part in the activities of the Society... As the A.C. seems to us no longer to have a *raison d'être*, having been almost completely inactive from 1931 to 1938, we consider that the most logical solution would be for it to dissolve."

This misses the point of the Academic Committee, though. It was not set up to include the general run of RSL Council members and vice-presidents; indeed, its main object, it would seem, was to exclude them. In 1910 they were mainly the remnants of the old guard from which Gosse, Newbolt and other AC activists wanted to distance themselves. Deliberately, they set themselves apart from run-of-the-mill members, creamed off the few who were distinguished and recruited from outside everyone else they considered distinguished. In effect, there were two RSLs, a high-powered one in the AC and a lowly one that occasionally showed spurts of resentment and low morale.

The AC had raised the profile of the RSL with its involvement of the great and the influential, and had done some of the things that should have been done throughout the nineteenth century. But in the long run, by its implicit snub to the less famous, it produced an unhealthy atmosphere, and the war provided the final good excuse to chop it down.

So was the Academic Committee just a snobbish attempt to get away from the dowdier elements of the RSL? Well, not "just", perhaps. Clearly there was a good deal of that about it. And if the end justifies the means (does it ever?), then it was probably justified. A decisive cut with the old guard meant that things could progress at a much higher level. In public esteem the RSL's image was immeasurably improved, and while the original activists were still active, things went well.

Everything changed, even the name of the published papers given at RSL meetings, and the format of the new volumes. No longer called *Transactions*, as they had been for the past century, they now had a name that to modern ears has an unappealing sound: *Essays by Divers Hands*. The folksiness of that "divers" may recall the arts and crafts movement, which was at its height at around the time, and was often reflected in current speech. Each volume contains six papers or so, and an introduction by the editor, who changed each time and was almost invariably a member of the Academic Committee. The first volume appeared in 1921, edited by Newbolt, the next the following year, edited by the literary churchman William Inge, Dean of St Paul's. Subsequent editors, all "names", included Chesterton, Gosse, Drinkwater, Binyon, Hugh Walpole, de la Mare, Francis Younghusband, Edward Marsh, Angela Thirkell and Harold Nicolson, whose refusal to join the Academic Committee had made no difference to his Fellowship, which he kept until his death in 1968.

But in the middle of the war, in 1916, something else emerged: another committee; indeed, a whole series of committees each descended from another so that they made a kind of family tree. The main one, grandfather of all the rest, may have owed its existence to the AC because, without the famous names now on it, outsiders would probably not have taken the RSL seriously enough to use it as an umbrella for its wide-ranging, grandiose plans. One cannot imagine the obscure old-time Society, intent on its own affairs, considering them, or outsiders wanting to cooperate with it if it had done so.

The new committee and those it spawned were more widely influential than the AC; their aims were broader, worthier, more idealistic. Although many of the members overlapped between the old and the new (the ubiquitous Gosse and Newbolt, for instance), there was little of the old exclusiveness and petty oneupmanship. The object of the new committees was no less than the promotion of a cultural bond, in every European country and then around the globe; the establishment of a band of brothers, ingenuously but attractively envisaged as able to change not just the ways of the world — its outlook, its behaviour, its politics — but the hearts and spirits of those around it; an idealistic vision, greathearted if unachievable, of a global community totally unlike the one that had made possible the terrible war then raging. Things had to change, and the way to change them was through cultural cooperation. It seems breathtakingly simple, even simple-minded; absurdly hopeful in a way one can only consider tenderly. Today, it would certainly not be possible to find so many taking it all seriously.

[61]

The name of the new body was cumbersome, but it was not an age of soundbites: the Committee of the Royal Society of Literature for Promoting an Intellectual Entente among the Allied and Friendly Countries, known very soon as the Entente Committee. Allied and Friendly meant everyone except Germany, a figure of unspeakable evil in 1916, completely excluded from any plans for the postwar world (hence Versailles, and all that followed it). It meant countries far away as well as in Europe; the whole of the British Empire (not surprisingly), which covered between a quarter and a third of the globe; what was called the Orient (Far and Near East); Russia (the Revolution was still to come); North America; and even South America, though contact there was patchy and haphazard.

The members of the Entente Committee were high-powered and wide-ranging, from Balfour, then Foreign Secretary, to Hardy, from Gilbert Murray to Lord Crewe and the Public Orator at Cambridge. Its aims were far-reaching but at first quite modestly expressed. As confidence grew, they became more ambitious. Francis Young-husband, then chairman of the sub-committee for Oriental countries, enlarged on Gosse's manifesto: "At the present time," he writes, "nothing less than the reconstitution of civilisation is actually proceeding under our very eyes. The life of nations has been so intensified, and the colossal suffering caused by the conflict has so deepened the craving of the nations for deeper harmony, that we may well believe that in the course of years the intellectual entente we now desire to promote may gradually develop into an intel-lectual union of the nations; that this union of culture may in its turn unite with similar unions of industry and science, and all these with a political union of free nations; and that the whole may be embodied in some Universal Institution empowered by the several nations to hold humanity together, direct its course, and be the means of ensuring that each nation, and thereby each individual, should have the greatest degree of freedom to develop its own life in its own way.

"Our present need is precise knowledge of each other: character, temperament and outlook; and more particularly of what we are each thinking and doing... we hope that each may be imbued and penetrated with some part of the culture of all the others and that every nation will contribute some element of the general culture. A mutual emulation after perfection will thus be set up. Each will seek to reach and surpass the best in the other." Others had similar dreams and laid similar plans. Despite the horrors, it was for many a time of almost lyrically expressed hope and confidence.

The Entente Committee was the main one, with Balfour its chairman. Around or below it, sub-committees sprang up, one for each friend and ally. British friends and allies served on these, and even in wartime there was much to-ing and fro-ing between Britain and the relevant country, and between its academics and committee members at home or on the move: conferencing, exchanges, cross-country politeness and an air of strong international interest and cooperation. Never did the RSL seem closer to foreign lands, friends and literatures. Its lectures and medals reflect this: papers on the Romantic age in Italian literature,

Modern Hindustani drama, Góngora, Rhythm in English and Italian poetry, Dante and Boethius; medals to Maurice Barrès, Harald Nielsen, Galdós, Valdés.

The Anglo-Foreign Societies came together in a permanent committee. These societies covered a large portion of the world (although the Empire was not counted as foreign): there were the Anglo-French, Anglo-Norse, Anglo-Roumanian, Anglo-Portuguese and Brazilian, Anglo-Spanish; China, Japan, Persian and Serbian Societies; the Anglo-Hellenic and British-Italian Leagues; the Anglo-Belgian Union, the Entente Cordiale, the Anglo-Italian Literary Society, the United Russia Societies Association (soon to be disbanded in revolution), and committees on relations with Oriental countries and the USA. All these have boxes of occasionally rewarding papers, busy over all sorts of things: establishing professorships, distributing English books abroad, discussing the teaching of science or modern languages, welcoming strangers, making reports, giving dinners, endlessly writing letters and setting up more sub-committees.

The main one of these was the Education Committee, with its sub-sub-offshoot, the Civic and Moral Education Committee, a more didactic affair. It is hard to be sure what, with all their meetings and high hopes, these achieved. What is certain, though, is that they produced a great deal of goodwill at a time when "friendly", that is, neutral, countries like Spain or those of Scandinavia had little official connection, beyond the strictly diplomatic, with British institutions. The appointment of honorary RSL correspondents in other countries brought closer ties with them and no doubt a flattering sense of their being involved in matters beyond their own frontiers. These correspondents (always someone of the country's nationality, not a British expatriate) were sometimes very distinguished: Spain's, for instance, was for some years Salvador de Madariaga, whose knowledge of Britain and excellent English (written, anyway), as well as his position in the world of letters, were exactly what was needed; and the file on Anglo-Spanish relations shows how fruitful these links between Spain and the RSL became.

All this suggests the RSL had a more important, certainly a wider, role than it had had before or was to have later. In 1918 spirits were high and hopeful, a new world seemed to be opening up. "I am glad things look so promising as regards the RSL," someone wrote to Newbolt that year. Stylistically and in its attitudes, the letter sounds like Younghusband's, but with something unsigned you cannot be sure. "...through the organisation now established [he writes on Entente Committee paper] an influence of unlimited power is made possible. You admit this, at least mentally. The time will come when the truth of it will take on a religious warmth, not only here but still more in other countries."

Today, this rhetoric may seem far-fetched, and even Gosse's aims may be pitched too high, but their ideas prefigure those of the League of Nations and later of the United Nations: a world community, the power of international understanding, the brotherhood of man. The more prosaic plans of the Education Committee were also much like those of the British Council, which began in the Thirties and still flies the flag around the world in similar ways, carrying out educational schemes the RSL first thought of: scholarships, exchanges, libraries, spreading a knowledge of British culture and acquiring that of others. The task was too big for a single, private organisation like the RSL, without funds for anything beyond goodwill and social effort. It needed government backing, large-scale spending, world-wide contacts, a whole organisational network.

It seemed possible that the British Council would remember its not very distant forebear in the RSL. I asked and hoped, but drew a blank: there was no mention of it in the Council's official history, no-one today had ever heard of it, even as a rumour nothing had filtered down to show how closely the RSL's international ideas and ambitions resem-bled its own. Archives show two things, mainly: how much, often trivial, is recorded and remembered and how quickly much else, often important, is forgotten and lost.

Even if there was no direct line of influence from the Entente activities to the British Council, and even if every-one has forgotten all about the earlier ones, there may have been some subterranean communication, a memory in the mid-Thirties of what had been hoped for, if not implemented, only ten or fifteen years earlier. Lord Crewe, so active in the RSL, so distinguished in public life, seems a likely link. At least the atmosphere was prepared, the international scene set, even the ideals expressed and perhaps believed in. We cannot know. What is now needed is a study and an analysis of what happened. Certainly the First World War and its aftermath seems to have been the RSL's finest hour.

HEADQUARTERS

AN INSTITUTION'S home is as important as a person's. It shows the personality, the taste, the status of the institution, its care for its image, its current state of prosperity, everything. The home's permanence or impermanence has an effect on all that happens in it and on everyone who works there. The RSL has had its years of good fortune and its lean years, large fine buildings and cramped, shared premises with every sort of disadvantage. What now seem foolish decisions and failures to take the long view have added to its later cares and difficulties. What seem to be dreadful purchases and mismanagement of funds in the 1870s are skimmed over in the minutes of Council meetings, but large sums were clearly lost and no one seems to have been held responsible.

"If anyone conversant with the needs of a Society were asked what was the greatest blow it could sustain, he would reply: the loss of a local habitation," Miss Rudston Brown, the Secretary, said in a broadcast in 1945. "Since 1884 [when it was turned out of its own house by the government] the Society has had to be content with temporary tenancies. That the blow was not fatal is due to the continuity of Literature as a spiritual power, for things of the spirit do not succumb under material disadvantage. Moreover, Literature accompanies Man in every walk of life, just as a pleasant brook might flow beside his dusty path, at times playing over the pebbles and shallows of wit and laughter, and then again deepening into quiet pools of meditation and wisdom, but ever beside him, the friend and comforter of his soul." Miss Rudston Brown is hard not to warm to, particularly when she is in lyrical vein.

It is pleasant to think that the RSL's first address is unchanged today. Other places it occupied have been given other uses or even, like the first, indeed the only, house it ever owned, 4 St Martin's Place, knocked down. But its original home — scarcely that: more a *poste restante*, but also a toehold in a wider world — was at Hatchards bookshop, then as now at 187 Piccadilly. In 1797 the young John Hatchard, still in his twenties but with fifteen years' experience of bookselling behind him, bought a bookshop (already a going concern) at 173 Piccadilly. By 1821, when the first letters for the RSL arrived there, it had moved twice, always within the same small area: in 1801 to larger premises at 190 Piccadilly, in 1817 to number 187, where it remains today.

Hatchards was then much more than a bookshop. Its founder was a publisher as well as a bookseller, and his firm continued to publish political and religious pamphlets until the 1880s. From the beginning he was able to attract not only the royal family (Queen Charlotte's name appears in the first of his sales ledgers) but many prominent men of the day, who met in the shop's cosy back room, with its armchairs and fire, for coffee, smoking and conversation. Meetings must have been leisurely, as there were benches for the servants of those inside to sit waiting for them in the street. The atmosphere and function of the place were like those of an eighteenth-century coffee house, somewhere for the bookish, the political, the cultivated of all sorts to meet and exchange views; a small-scale gentlemen's club, in fact.

It was there that early discussions about the RSL took place. Jerdan mentions several in his autobiography, the earliest very soon after Burgess's visit to Carlton House to be told about the setting up of the RSL (the king sent for him on 2 November 1820; the meeting at Hatchards took place on 20 November). Four days after that, a notice, already headed "Royal Society of Literature, Instituted under the Patronage, and endowed by the Munificence, of THE KING", went out announcing "Premiums for the Years 1821 and 1822". These were prizes offered for a poem and dissertations. The notice was signed T. Yeates, with "Committee Room, at Messrs Hatchards', Piccadilly, Monday, December 4th, 1820" at the bottom of the page. Yeates later argued with the Council over his salary, so the Reverend Richard Cattermole, a writer of sorts and brother of the artist George Cattermole, occasional illustrator of Dickens, was appointed Secretary at the first General Meeting and served for the next three decades. Both he and Yeates were later helped by the Literary Fund, which showed its goodwill towards the newly founded RSL as early as 1823, when Sir Benjamin Hobhouse, vice-president of the Fund and chairman of its committee, wrote suggesting "that the use of the apartments of the Literary Fund be offered to the Royal Society of Literature".

Early in its history, even before it received its Charter of Incorporation, the Society decided it must make provision for a home of its own. The first General Meeting — what would now be called an AGM — took place at the "House of the Literary Fund Society" in Lincoln's Inn Fields. There the Council was "authorised... to take the requisite steps to provide a suitable place for the Society's regular meetings" and Cattermole was asked to arrange for weekly meetings of the Council to be held in the Librarian's room at the British Museum, where papers would be read and business conducted. By the next anniversary meeting, in May 1824, the Society had a home of its own, 61 Lincoln's Inn Fields, a few houses away from its friends at the Literary Fund.

The following year Burgess said in his presidential address that the RSL needed "a permanent house, or apartments, of more convenient situation and more adequate to the wants of the Society, than what [they occupied] at present". What they then occupied were still the rooms in Lincoln's Inn Fields, but by the following February they had moved from its cramped quarters to others at 2 Parliament Street, close to the Palace of Westminster but also "barely sufficient for the accommodation of the Society". Good news, though, came two months later, in April: the king was "pleased to direct an allotment of land to be given to the Society", as indeed Burgess, the previous year, had hinted he might do.

The Royal Society of Literature Building Fund was then launched. John Nash, the king's architect, wanted the RSL site to be part of a larger plan. What is now Trafalgar Square was made by clearing away the Royal Mews and other buildings on the east and west sides, and Nash proposed a single house that would contain the Athenaeum club, St Martin's Vicarage, and the RSL. In the event both the Athenaeum and the RSL were housed elsewhere, and Decimus Burton designed buildings for them both — a large grand one in Pall Mall for the Athenaeum and a more modest one in St Martin's Place, where the National Portrait Gallery is now, not far from Nash's original site, for the RSL. It is pleasant to think of this area, set in "teeming London's central roar", being the responsibility of the Commissioners of Roads and Forests.

Anyone buying or building a house today will sympathise with the RSL over the next few years: over delays and disappointments, frustrations and changes of plan, red tape. It was not until 7 March, 1830, that the *Sunday Times* made an announcement: "The Royal Society of Literature are [sic], it is said, to have a site assigned to them out of the vacant space near St Martin's Church for their new building." Things then rushed ahead. The Society expected to take over its new house by the following November at latest. The ground floor was to be let to the Incorporated Society for the Building and Enlargement of Churches and Chapels (how Betjeman would have enjoyed the conjunction of those two bodies!). The minutes of the General Anniversary Meeting tell the tale, in a rather livelier manner than usual: "The Council having, shortly after the General Meeting of 1830, obtained, on a lease of ninety-nine years, from the Commissioners of Roads and Forests, a piece of ground for the site of the proposed House for the Society, in the Vicinity of St Martin's Church, proceeded to commence the Building without further delay. A beautiful design was gratuitously furnished by Mr Decimus Burton, whom the council had appointed their Architect... The Council have the satisfaction of informing the Meeting, that the building is now far advanced towards completion."

Minutes of RSL meetings are generally so dry that even the use of the adjective "beautiful" or of a phrase like "the Council have the satisfaction" sounds fulsome. At long last the Society had its own home, designed without charge by one of the leading architects of the day, a handsome house which must have given it prestige and self confidence.

Was the RSL given its land by the king, as the earlier statements seem to imply? Or does the reference to "applications to be allowed to purchase sufficient ground" mean it had to be paid for? By the time the final transactions were in hand George IV had just died. William IV was conspicuously less generous to the RSL, causing hardship to the Associates as well as ill feeling in the Society. Perhaps he withdrew the present of land as well as the pensions. Details are now hard if not impossible to come by; but whatever they were, the General Anniversary Meeting of 1832 was held in the Society's own home, to the huzzas of the Council. Decimus Burton generously paid his fee of £146.16s into the Building Fund. The second floor was let, first to Sir Thomas Phillips, an old RSL friend, at £100 a year, and then to the Statistical Society at 100 guineas. A touching letter from Sir Thomas explains how, since his wife's death, he cannot bear to live in the place which reminds him of her, or to look out of the window at the trees she used to see.

So there was the RSL, installed in its own house for the next half century.

For some years before it happened the Society had known that it would have to move out of its first proper home. The government wanted the site for a building which would house the portraits then held in the National Gallery, and the National Portrait Gallery as it now stands was built after Decimus Burton's house had been demolished. Later, the RSL's apparent lack of any struggle to stay there was criticised. Strangely, though, the remarkable turnabout in the Society's fortunes began eleven years after its loss of a permanent home, and what now seem its golden years from 1907 to the Thirties took place in the wilderness of short leases, shared houses and uncertainty.

We do not know the details of negotiations that must have taken place up to 1884, how determined the government was, how weak the Council may have been. All this might make an interesting tale if it were known. Certainly the next sixty-five years, when the RSL wandered from one inadequate lodging to another, cannot have been a satisfactory time. The end of its ownership of a house came on 29 September 1884. The previous year had seen the usual scurry that house-hunting involves, the raising and dashing of hopes, the discussions, the financial worries. Houses in Bedford Square in Bloomsbury, Arlington Street off Piccadilly, and St James's Place, off St James's Street, a little nearer Green Park, were seen and considered; and no doubt others. Some were too expensive, some too dilapidated, one was too "far east", whatever that meant. Finally, a place to let was found in a street that no longer exists, close to what is now Bridge Street, in Westminster, although on the die-stamped RSL paper the location is given as Green Park.

[73]

The rent was £250 a year, a housekeeper was to be paid 10/6 a week, and gas would cost what sounds like the tiny sum of £1 a year; the lease was for five and three quarter years (though it was finally stretched to six) and the RSL was to return the rooms in their original condition.

In the minutes, De la Hay Street was mentioned with that spelling; but on the RSL paper and a single envelope I have found addressed to it there, it has become Delahay Street. The now vanished street and the RSL's six years there seem somehow to have been mislaid in the records, and accounts of the Society's doings say that the move was directly from St Martin's Place to Hanover Square, where it stayed for the next twenty-five years, until 1915.

At the beginning of the new century there were already moves afoot to find somewhere else. The minutes of Council meetings are hard to fathom, so brisk and uncommunicative are they, but in 1907 there is talk of "new premises" and in 1908 of "large numbers" of rooms being looked at. Certainly the accommodation in Hanover Square seems to have been dingy. "The present quarters of the RSL are inconvenient, inadequate, badly situated and exceedingly expensive," wrote the Secretary, Percy Ames. "The approach is mean and undignified; the Society has exclusive use of *one room* only and has no space to accommodate gifts which would add importance, interest and prestige." Throughout 1914 and the first half of 1915 there were longwinded but friendly

4 St Martin's Place
Designed by Decimus Burton, the home of the Royal Society of Literature (second from left) from 1830-1884

[74]

discussions about arrangements in Hanover Square: the moving of books, the removal of furniture, box-and-cox use of the rooms and, most importantly, a reduction in the rent. Negotiations at last collapsed and the RSL gave notice, arranging to pay £300 to cancel the remainder of the lease.

A house in Russell Square belonging to the Royal Historical Society was to become its new home; all was arranged, but at the last minute the building was found to be alarmingly unsafe, and the RSL was asked to pay for shoring it up; also, the lease was only three years long and the RSL wanted a minimum of five. So the original landlords were asked if they would have the Society back in Hanover Square, but they said no, the rooms had already been let to someone else. A rather hurried move was made to Number 2, Bloomsbury Square, the headquarters of the College of Preceptors (trainers of teachers, suppliers of certificates to schools before the Oxford and Cambridge boards ran public examinations, and today still running educational services and courses for teachers, though no longer from Bloomsbury Square). "Two good rooms on ground floor to be let at £200 inclusive of lighting, firing, cleaning and attendance" is how the minutes describe the new premises.

And there, for the next thirty-four years, the RSL stayed.

Plans to move, to acquire a home of its own — if not freehold, at least independent — continued. In the Twenties and Thirties the idea was still very much in people's minds. Andrew Carnegie was approached for help, and the Pilgrim Trust (both unsuccessfully). With the Second World War, plans for a move were put aside.

After the war, it was decided to look again, and by 1948 the househunt was in full swing. For months Council, RSL officers and the president looked at houses in central London, mostly at elegant addresses, although the buildings themselves cannot then have been very elegant: war damage had still to be put right in almost every London house and people would now find it hard to imagine the shabbiness of the streets. It was not just bombing, fire damage and the ragged growth of all kinds of vegetation that made them so decrepit, but lack of everyday care for nearly a decade. Two houses were looked at in Belgrave Square (one is today the Italian Institute of Culture), one in Cadogan Square, one in Cottesmore Gardens, one in The Boltons. Finally, in November 1948, the house which was to become the RSL headquarters in 1950 was considered.

Number 1, Hyde Park Gardens, a large handsome house, was the home of General Sir Ian Hamilton (of Gallipoli fame, or notoriety) until his death in 1947. In an article in *News of the Royal Society of Literature* of November 1997, shortly before his death, James Lees-Milne, a Fellow who knew the Hamiltons well, described the house as it had been in their day. He also wrote to me in August 1997 about his connections with the RSL and the house. He describes how Lady Hamilton (known to him as Aunt Jean) had in 1913 knocked "five stuffy rooms on the ground floor into a single oddly-shaped reception hall from one end of which rose a great staircase". Roger Fry had helped with this transformation, which later made the house so suitable for the RSL. The oddly-shaped room became its lecture hall and the great staircase had the advantage of being available when the room was overcrowded for popular lectures: people could sit up the stairs in cosy rows. For special occasions, too, nightlights were placed very prettily on each step, gleaming through the iron banisters on to the two full-length lifesize portraits of the handsome, soldierly Sir Ian which still hung on the staircase wall.

"The whole was decorated in sombre black and jade green," Lees-Milne wrote of the old house. "Bought from the Omega Workshops, mosaics adorned the floor and stained glass the windows. ... When the austere poet Robert Bridges first climbed the majestic staircase he asked his host tersely, 'Who built this pretentious house?' 'My wife,' came the reply."

Those who first saw the house in Hyde Park Gardens, admittedly in its shabby unfurnished postwar condition, failed to notice its possibilities. Miss Rudston Brown, still Secretary, says it "appears admirable in all respects except financial" (the rent of £500 a year seemed excessive). Obviously she thought well of it, but there was no delighted reaction in her report. Perhaps she had recently seen too many splendid houses in much grander places than W2; "north of the Park" was not yet considered a "good address". No one mentions the house's attractiveness or its potential beauty after redecoration; no one seems to have an aesthetic opinion about it at all. Lord Wavell stuck to mild approval and practicalities: "The situation is good, looking south over Hyde Park. It is easily accessible by bus

The entrance to 1 Hyde Park Gardens, the RSL's home from 1950-1999

[78]

or tube. The accommodation on the Ground and First floors is ample for our purpose. Whether we require the Basement I do not know. There is quite a large terrace in front of the house, between it and the Park, which might be useful for tea in the summer months." (Miss Rudston Brown, like Gosse, disapproved of afternoon tea, so perhaps not.)

CELEBRATIONS

F UN AND games may not be the top priority in a professional society, but celebrations are a memorable part of life and give a fillip to the morale of any organisation. Over the years the RSL has celebrated awards, honours, anniversaries, foreign and occasionally royal visits, special occasions of every sort. These leave a trail of scuffed mementos which with the years look forlorn: programmes, menus, bills, letters, frantic last-minute telegrams and occasionally angry complaints of gate-crashing and rudeness and lost umbrellas.

The grander occasions have left photograph albums and boxes recording events that are generally undated, sometimes unidentified, with pictures of forgotten Fellows, now forever unidentifiable because everyone who knew them has died, in clothes that to more modern eyes look hideous, with startled expressions and terrible hats. As portraits these snaps taken in mid-sentence or mid-bite are probably closer to life than the studio photographs on dust-jackets, which are often decades out of date, black-haired instead of white, slim instead of stout, the features composed to face the world at their best.

More modest celebrations took place every month (in ten out of the yearly twelve, anyway), with a lecture and then a party. 1, Hyde Park Gardens had room for quite large numbers and after a talk wine was served and the lecturer was available for discussion and chat with the audience. Fellows' lunches, popular and well attended, were another kind of celebration. Each month (or again, in ten months out of twelve) about twenty Fellows came together, with one of them, a new one each month, as host. A writer's life can be solitary and a chance to meet one's peers in a leisurely way, not just standing about with a drink, is often welcome. Excellent food, an attractively laid large table, the panelled Council room with the garden outside, Bishop Burgess under his glass dome, place and people: all added up to an enjoyable regular ritual. Other celebrations were evening literary events for which outsiders hired the ground floor: book launches, prize givings, gatherings of publishers and writers and magazines for birthdays or anniversaries, bookish occasions of all sorts. The high rooms were transformed, often with spotlights and other special effects, with drapery and flowers, greenery, even trees. Visitors were amazed to find such an Aladdin's cave in central London. Television and radio programmes were sometimes made in the house — because of either its beauty or its associations, or both.

Regular award ceremonies were held, and will continue to be held, for two annual prizes; a third prize has recently been set up (for a short story, in memory of V.S. Pritchett). The Heinemann award, now worth £5000, was established in the early 1940s from a bequest of the publisher William Heinemann, and is given to what the judges consider the best book in any genre, preferably (he suggested) one unlikely to have popular appeal. Poetry, criticism, memoirs, travel, biography, history, fiction: all have been Heinemann

1 Hyde Park Gardens

[82]

winners, and sometimes the prize is divided between two or three. More modest, at £1000, is the Winifred Holtby award, set up by Vera Brittain in memory of her friend who died in 1935 at the age of thirty-seven. The award is for a provincial, or regional, novel, and Vera Brittain probably had in mind something similar to Winifred Holtby's last and best work, the posthumously published *South Riding*, a classic provincial novel set in a single, closely examined place, with *Middlemarch* its great ancestor. But today, with television and travel and restlessness, such places, such ways of life, scarcely exist, and the true provincial novel scarcely exists either. So the terms of the award have become vaguer, and a novel "with a strong sense of a particular place" is now eligible for the prize.

Another award is the Benson medal, set up in 1916 by A.C. Benson for poetry, fiction, history, biography and *belles-lettres*. This is awarded irregularly, more often for the writer's work as a whole than for a single book. The medals, of solid silver and nearly three inches across, were first awarded to foreign writers; so were the last four (to Wole Soyinka, Julien Green, Naguib Mahfouz and Shusako Endo). The other twenty-four Benson medals have gone to British writers and the ceremonies at which they were handed over were often grand affairs, as old photographs show. Grandest of all, and deservedly so, were those at which the Society's gold medals were given. These were something rare and special; until 1961, when the award of Companion of Literature was instituted for a lifetime's work, they were the RSL's highest honour. Scott was given one by the king who so much admired him, as a heartfelt and personal tribute. After a long gap they were given to Hardy, Meredith and Kipling, and in 1939 to Shaw.

Anniversaries provide an excuse for celebration and with so many writers, dead or alive, to choose from, dates of birth and death come round frequently. Every Fellow's introduction is of course a celebration. But the biggest applause today goes to the installation of Companions of Literature. The first four, in 1961, at the Skinners' Hall, were Churchill, Forster, Maugham and Masefield. The latter two, looking painfully ancient in the surviving photographs, managed to get to the party, the former each sent a deputy to collect his scroll.

Celebrations for special dates and occasions involve enormous hidden efforts by RSL staff and, to a lesser degree, officers. In 1925 the centenary of the RSL was commemorated with a dinner (the date, as I have said, was five years out), and fifty years later (again five years out) the 150th anniversary had a more imaginative commemoration with a poetry reading, again at the Skinners' Hall, attended by the Queen. For the seeker of long-forgotten truths the most interesting part of this kind of event is not the smooth result, the faultless performance on the night, but the scurrying behind the scenes before and after. Lady Birkenhead, the president's wife, decides that ladies must wear long dresses, but that gloves are optional. Guests are to be given Veuve de Vernay, but *proper* champagne for the Queen's room. We have checked on this" [the Secretary goes on] "and she wants it". Then there are the details: orders of precedence in presenting guests to the Queen, thank-you letters (the same rather gushing one to all the poetry readers), expenses paid to them, and (again inevitably) the lost parcel, which Lord David Cecil, when asked, denies he carried off.

The Queen's presence seems to have overwhelmed some of the guests. Rebecca West, not usually an effusive woman, wrote to Mrs Patterson, the RSL Secretary, who had sent her a photograph: "You thought I would like this. I do! I do! 'Beauty and the Beast' it might be entitled. And what beauty it is! And what niceness, what discipline to be so nice when it is so often required to be nice, and what luck for England that the House of Hanover, which sometimes does not flower, has produced *this* flower." The Beast was Lord Butler, the age of the Beauty, thus florally celebrated, forty-nine. Buckingham Palace (on first-name terms) writes to tell Lord Butler "how tremendously she had enjoyed the poetry reading", but one of the poetry readers wonders afterwards if in fact she had ("All she talked about with me was the Skinners' Hall!"). These affairs inevitably have their risks and disappointments, their foolish little hurts ("Poor Bridget didn't even get in a curtsey.").

Then there are one-off events and worldly excitements which involve the RSL. At the Coronation party in the garden of 10 Downing Street in 1953 the Birkenheads, the Butlers, Edith Sitwell, Freya Stark and Edith Evans are all found (in curling photographs), with Lawrence Olivier

9 December 1975: The Queen at the celebration of the founding of the RSL (mistakenly supposed to be the 150th anniversary), with from left, Rebecca West, Angus Wilson, C.V. Wedgwood, Mrs Mollie Patterson (Secretary of the RSL) and Lord Butler

among them. Foreign visitors are entertained, sometimes lavishly. The Canadian Authors Association (which has a large boxfile devoted to arrangements for its visit) had the unusual honour of a speech from Kipling at its luncheon — unusual because it was broadcast and this was the only time Kipling agreed to speak on the wireless. In the days when radio had an audience which, though much smaller, was the nearest equivalent to that for television today, the broadcast brought the RSL much public notice.

Finally, or perhaps not finally, because they seem endless, there are the great events which the RSL has, if not quite to celebrate, at least to mark, write letters about, put in a polite appearance at. These are births, deaths and marriages, often royal. The box of royal papers makes fascinating social history, the tone changing a little down the years, from stately and humble (by modern standards grovelling) to a little less stately, but not much. William IV has the sympathy of the President and Council on the death of their "late revered Sovereign" and then congratulations on his accession (much good it did them, since he immediately cancelled all his brother's financial help). Queen Alexandra has condolences from the Fellows, who "assure Her Majesty of their respectful and devoted interest in everything that affects her happiness" (Coleridge's grandson signs this unlikely assurance). Queen Victoria is consoled after the deaths of various relatives, and congratulated on her diamond jubilee and

Farewell to Hyde Park Gardens, 25 November 1999.
Lord Jenkins cuts the cake, a culinary pastiche of 'Essays by Divers Hands',
with Michael Holroyd

on the birth of a great-grandson (the future Edward VIII). Occasionally, even on such stately occasions, someone trips up: on the death of Prince Albert in 1862 the royal reply to the RSL's condolences is addressed to the Bishop of St David's, who had died twenty-five years earlier and in any case had been Bishop of Salisbury, not St David's, since 1825, nearly forty years before.

At the partygoing level, modern style, there are the royal garden parties, to which each summer four RSL Fellows are invited, taking, if they have them and want to, an indefinite number of unmarried daughters under the age of twenty-five. How delighted those Victorian families of daughters might have been, the Potters with their nine girls, Sir Thomas Fowler with (I think) his eleven, the charmingly named Bishop Sheepshanks with a brood so numerous they were often mistaken for a girls' school crocodile, or, bending the rules a little, Lewis Carroll with all those sisters, boxed up together in everlasting spinsterhood at The Laurels, Guildford.

ONWARDS

ND SO, for lack of space (though not of interest — mine, or in the material), I must end this brief account; a portrait, or indeed a series of snapshots, rather than a history. Exactly upon the millennium, and exactly fifty years after it came to its present home, the RSL is set for a new life in a new place, where a new portrait will be needed. A detailed history from the large archive will take much longer.

Plunging into the detail — sometimes intimate — of lives and behaviour decades ago has been strange and stimulating. The whole story is not, of course, only about the clash or confluence of personalities. Large issues, world affairs, the atmosphere of the time, the social set-up, politics and economics all had their effect. It is hard to separate the personal from the general, the detail from the whole. But institutions repay study, having at least two layers of reality, the official and the unknown, the unacknowledged. Documents tell both stories. The official one is found in all those minutes and reports, records with little colour and few personal details or asides. The unofficial lies in the letters and memos, anecdotes, memoirs, gossip; in those boxes of curling photographs, bills, complaints, tales of ill-health and poverty and grievance, of stolen umbrellas and missing hats, of gout and intemperance, misbehaviour, political incorrectness, social history of every sort. Both kinds of history are needed: dignified narrative in the official tale, but little verve or individuality; more fun and fizz in the subcutaneous, but sometimes indiscretion and dubious frills.

Nearly every institutional history (like many biographies) has a volcanic centre of rows, resentments, even violence; certainly of differences, enmities, dislikes and discourtesies. Factions, allegiances and cabals all flourish; established friendships founder, often irrevocably. When an outspoken history of any institution is written, this is often clearly the case; or else, reading between the lines of pious and nervous discretion, it seems equally likely to be so. In most learned societies people from time to time clash furiously on matters of principle, organisation, finance, or individual power and prestige; they quarrel over buildings, or the form of committees, or (as we have seen) whether or not to serve afternoon tea. Above all they have their hackles raised by intangible, unmentionable things like atmosphere, politeness, social nuances, class. This is human nature in a confined space, enclosed in a narrow, often jealous world; it is the politics of power in action. It is also the more attractive world of like-minded people who get together for the benefit of themselves and others, to advance the cause of what they most value — their work; who enjoy meetings and exchanges, promote the welfare of their kind, relish reminiscence and celebration; the sociable, the clubbable, those who like talking shop.

Literary life suggests literary comparisons. In looking through the papers I sometimes felt I was living in a novel by Muriel Spark, so bizarre yet so credible were events and feelings. With a particular mad cleric, who has a large box file to himself, I was clearly going through a text-book case of advanced self-delusion, jealousy and rage; when he got his come-uppance it was almost Malvolio-like in its sad absurdity. And in a touching and occasionally almost tender case, showing the prim relationship between two lonely-sounding colleagues, male and female, over several decades in which their first names were never once revealed, I was reminded of *84 Charing Cross Road*. Fiction and fact often seemed to overlap, but history is not fiction, so guesswork was not in order. As I have said, mistakes of fact or ambiguous tales in the RSL's past have been repeated down the years and anyone trying to discover what happened over nearly two centuries must apologise in advance for gaps and grey areas. Probably no malice or cover-up is involved, simply the acceptance of what others have said, who have accepted what earlier others have said, and so on back to 1820. Collecting the evidence is like trying to put downy feathers in a bag; it flies about, often bedraggled, incompetent to provide anything like a complete history of the past.

Is this because of carelessness, theft, house-moves, surreptitious sales, war damage, ignorance, or a combination of several? Peter Hennessy has told how, since Britain has an unwritten constitution, documents vital to government vanish into cupboards, presumably someone's "safe place", later forgotten. When in 1982 there was a question of war being declared on Argentina, the papers describing exactly how a declaration was made had disappeared. Twelve years later they turned up at the back of a particularly remote cupboard, strangely Pooter-like documents unseen since

1939. How exactly this reminded me of my hunts in the RSL cupboards.

But this is all in the past. The RSL cupboards, shelves and boxes were crammed and the history they held was rewarding, sometimes exemplary, sometimes fascinating. But what of the present? The RSL now seems in good shape, hopeful, energetic, dynamic, and on the brink of an expanding future. What are its activities today and its plans for tomorrow? They are what is called, in schoolboy's essay parlance, many and various. The RSL has always been busy with literary matters outside its immediate circle but perhaps never so much as it is now. It still carries out George IV's original plans, and, since its public-spirited days around and after the First World War, it has been involved in efforts of all kinds to advance literature and, more widely, education and international cooperation.

George IV's main plan for the RSL was the advancement of general literature. This it does through its lectures and meetings and its involvement in every worthwhile literary initiative. He wanted it to honour writers and reward literary merit. This it does by electing writers as Fellows and, from among them, choosing for special honour the Society's ten Companions of Literature; and through the yearly prizes which reward and encourage writers, often the young and unknown, in every genre. It makes official suggestions for the award of public honours, including the appointment of the Poet Laureate. But it is of interest, perhaps, that some writers value a Fellowship conferred by their peers more than a public honour decided upon by less literary civil servants.

The RSL gives writers, readers and the general public a chance to exchange views. Lectures are always followed by questions and discussion, and the parties afterwards are a modern, more open version of the salons of the past. The Society has established itself as a friendly centre for literary professionals, amateurs, enthusiasts, regular and irregular visitors of all sorts, nationalities and interests. In a practical way, it encourages new writers: an eighteenth-century cottage in Somerset, left to it by the Russian-born novelist E.M. Almedingen, is let at a low rent to a talented writer who needs it.

Literary initiatives put forward by other organisations have been and are still being supported by the RSL. It provided a platform in the campaign that led to Public Lending Right legislation, and was actively involved in the Hands Off Reading campaign which opposed the imposition of VAT on books. It has been a major sponsor of the eighteenth- and nineteenth-century *Location Register of English Literary Manuscripts and Letters* published in two volumes by the British Library in 1995, and of the two twentieth-century volumes (1988), the updating and revision of which it continues to support. It also supports WATCH (Writers and their Copyright Holders), a joint UK/USA project to build up on the Internet a database of those who hold the copyright of writers whose papers are housed in archives and manuscript repositories. Meanwhile the RSL has joined educational initiatives to improve the teaching of English in schools, to arrange workshops for schoolchildren, and to encourage Fellows to visit schools and give talks in them.

The RSL is concerned about the export of contemporary archives and manuscripts from Britain. With the Society of Authors, it is seeking ways to have the Heritage Lottery Fund guidelines changed so that funds are made available for the purchase of living writers' archives. It is also worried about the present low standard of publishers' editing, and has hosted discussions among authors, agents, publishers, and independent editorial consultants to find out how this problem may best be addressed. The Minister for the Arts has given the first of what it is hoped will be an annual address attended by representatives of other literary organisations. Finally the Society intends to strengthen its links with foreign writers.

All these projects ebbed and flowed as the RSL also began to confront the alarming though invigorating prospect of packing up and moving house at the end of 1999, when it had to leave Number 1, Hyde Park Gardens. If a change had to be made, the millennium — involving both fanfares and precision — seemed the right moment in which to make it. That house had beauty, grace and greenery, an atmosphere at once homely and rarefied, vistas of grass and trees and the frequent almost rural clop of horses' hooves in the road. 1 Hyde Park Gardens was elegant; the new home may be magnificent. After a few months in the offices of the Royal Literary Fund, which gave hospitality to the RSL in

Cambridge University Library
The Royal Society of Literature's archive has been housed there since 1999

its earliest days, the final move will take the RSL to a more central, Thames-side site, with echoes of Handel and touches of Canaletto, an atmosphere more urban and less domestic, and an address that in prestige, grandeur and history is perhaps the only one in London that can seem a worthy successor to its half-century-old occupation of 1 Hyde Park Gardens. And which is this paragon among buildings, newly and gorgeously appointed? None other than Somerset House.

ISABEL QUIGLY

Isabel Quigly was born in Spain and has lived in Sussex for many years. She has published a novel, *The Eye of Heaven* (Collins), called *The Exchange of Joy* in America (Harcourt Brace), and several books of criticism and social history; including *The Heirs of Tom Brown: the English school story* (Chatto & Windus; in paperback, OUP). She edited the Penguin Shelley, still in print after forty-five years, introduced and edited *Stalky & Co* in the World's Classics (OUP), and has translated about forty books, mostly from Italian, some from Spanish and French. For a decade she was the *Spectator*'s film critic and wrote *Charlie Chaplin: the early comedies* (Studio Vista; in USA, Dutton). Until recently, for twelve years, she was literary adviser to *The Tablet*. She is a Fellow of the Royal Society of Literature, and has served on its Council.

ACKNOWLEDGEMENTS

Many people gave me generous help with my researches. For much of what they shared with me I had, alas, not enough space, but it gave me a rich background against which to write and I hope to use more of it later. In particular I would like to thank Jill Balcon, Nina Bawden, Neville Braybrooke, Frank Chapman, Margaret Chester, James Fergusson, Christopher Fry, Alethea Hayter, Christopher Hibbert, Mary Hocking, Richard Holmes, Gerard Irvine, the late James Lees-Milne, Nigel Nicolson, Jacinta Nadal, the late Gillian Patterson, John Press, Jasper Ridley, June Robertson Rodger, Mary Stopes-Roe, Joan Tate, Ann Thwaite, Richard Usborne, A.N. Wilson, Joan Winterkorn. Also, from organisations, Sarah Bowman and Martin Higgs of Hatchards, Ursula Carlisle, archivist of the Mercers' Company, Paul Cox and Jacob Simon of the National Portrait Gallery, Clare Fleck, archivist at Knebworth, Gerald Fitzgerald of the Surrey National Trust, Jenny Haines of the College of Preceptors, Penny Herterich, Clerk to the Governors of the Central Foundation Schools of London, Peter Jackson of the London Topographical Society, Alexander Pullen of the British Museum, Canon William Price, archivist of St David's University College, Lampeter and the (alas, nameless) librarian at Lampeter. I would also like to thank the London Topographical Society for their permission to reproduce the print of St Martin's Place, and London Management who administer the estate of Max Beerbohm for permission to reproduce his cartoon of

[101]

members of the Academic Committee. Most of all my thanks to Maggie Fergusson, Elizabeth Hughes and Julia Abel Smith of the RSL, whose wonderful welcome made it a joy to work there and without whose help and friendliness I could never have got as far in the short space of time I was given.

Isabel Quigly